SLS Monograph

New subscribers to *Sign Language Studies* quickly discover the gems contained in back issues of the joural. Because many of the back issues of this quarterly journal are no longer available in print, readers have often requested that those gems be made available in a more convienient format. *SLS Monographs* is offered as a direct response to those requests. Each monograph will be devoted to a single topic and will select from pertinent articles that have appeared in *Sign Language Studies*. In some cases the articles will serve to trace the development of a particular line of theoretical inquiry and research. In other cases articles represent descriptive and empirical research on a given topic. *SLS Monographs* are useful as texts in Interpreter Education Programs, Sign Language classes, and Deaf Studies programs.

A portion of the proceeds from sales of *SLS Monographs* will be donated to the Stokoe Scholarship Fund. This scholarship is administered by the National Association of the Deaf. Scholarships are awarded annually to deaf graduate students to support their studies of Sign Language and/or the deaf community. Donations from proceeds will be made annually in the name of the authors whose work appears in this *SLS Monograph*.

For more information about the Stokoe Scholarship please contact the NAD. For more information about *Sign Language Studies*, the *SLS Monograph* series, and other scholarly publications on Sign Language and the deaf community contact:

Linstok Press
4020 Blackburn Lane
Burtonsville, MD 20866

ISBN 0-932130-12-7

SIGN LANGUAGE INTERPRETERS AND INTERPRETING

This *SLS Monograph* focuses on Sign Language interpreters and interpreting. The task of interpreting between two individuals or groups who share neither the same language nor the same culture is at once a challenging and humbling experience. All one need do is reflect on the frequecy of misunderstanding and miscommunication between individuals or groups who share the same language and culture to appreciate the enormous challenge faced by interpreters. Those who have interpreted betwen ASL and English, and have done so successfully, are surely humbled upon realizing that successful interpretation is as much a tribute to the desire of the participants to understand and be understood

The aritcles selected for this monograph all appeared in *Sign Language Studies* during a five year period of time from Winter 1986 through Spring 1991. Each article appears here as it was originally published. This enables readers to have direct access to these original works and to gain a sense of their historic and present day significance.

The original citation for each of the articles is as follows:

Subjective Assessment of Sign Language Interpreters
    SLS 53, Winter 1986
An Examination of Personal Characterisitcs & Abilities
    SLS 53, Winter 1986
Analysis of Changes in Interpreters' Language 1973-1985
    SLS 53, Winter 1986
Effects of Lag Time on Interpreter Errors
    SLS 53, Winter 1986

Determining Register in Sign-to-English Interpreting
        SLS 57, Winter 1987
Interpreters' Recognition of Structure & Meaning
        SLS 58, Spring 1988
Miscommunication in Interpreted Classroom
Interaction
        SLS 70, Spring 1991

In order to provide additional historical perspective, it is also helpful to repeat here the information about each author that appeared with the original articles.

Dennis Cokely - President of the Registry of
        Interpreters and President of Sign Media, Inc.
Steven Fritsch Rudser - a researcher and an
        interpreter at the Center on Deafness,
        University of California, San Francisco.
Robert Ingram - an employee of Hewlett Packard
        responsible for policy development and
        coordination.
Kristen Johnson - a doctoral candidate at the
        University of California, Los Angeles.
Risa Shaw - a student at George Mason University
Michael Strong - a research psychologist at the
        Center on Deafness, University of California,
        San Francisco.

For readers who are not interpreters, the perspectives in these articles provide an appreciation of the enormous challenges faced by Sign Language interpreters. For those readers who are interpreters or who aspire to become interpreters, these articles should serve as a sobering reminder of the need to attain the highest level of language skill and cultural sensitivity possible — and the consequences of failing to attain and maintain that skill and sensitivity.

                                        Dennis Cokely

I. THE SUBJECTIVE ASSESSMENT OF SIGN LANGUAGE INTERPRETERS

Michael Strong
Steven Fritsch Rudser

Abstract

A group of hearing raters were asked to make a subjective evaluation of the signed and spoken output of 25 sign language interpreters, using taped samples recorded under test conditions. Three hypotheses were examined: (1) that raters would agree with one another, (2) that subjective evaluations would correlate positively with interpreter accuracy ratings, and (3) that subjective raters would be able to determine whether the interpreters had deaf or hearing parents. Results showed that rater agreement was high (0.52 to 0.86) but much lower than would be required between raters on an objective measure. Correlation between subjective and objective assessment was also high (0.59 to 0.79). Subjects were not successful at identifying which interpreters had deaf parents. Implications are drawn for interpreter assessment in general, particularly that employed by the Registry of Interpreters for the Deaf.

Introduction

Training methods and assessment techniques are still at relatively early stages of development. Strong and Rudser (1985) have developed an instrument for the assessment of sign language interpreting skills that attempts to eliminate, as far as possible, the need for subjective decisions by the rater. It does so by focusing solely on the accuracy with which individual propositions are represented by the interpreter, thus reducing the number of value judgments a rater is required to make. Other existing techniques (e.g. that used by

1

the Registry of Interpreters for the Deaf) involve considerable subjective evaluation and thus are more open to the possibility of rater bias. While it may be desirable to have a measure of objective evaluation, subjective evaluations are being made all the time by teachers, trainers, students, and the deaf and hearing interlocutors for whom the interpreters work. It is therefore of some importance to examine the process of subjective evaluation, particularly by consumers (as they will have considerable influence on which interpreters are requested for particular tasks), in order to learn those aspects of an interpre-ter's performance that may be most salient in determining the rater's evaluations, and whether subjective evaluations are likely to be at variance with more objective assessments of the same people.

For many years social psychologists have been interested in the processes by which impressions, opinions, or feelings about other persons are formed. Frequently judgments are made about an individual based on minimal information, such as the sound of a voice, physical appearance, or a self-written resume. In such cases, the perceiver is frequently influenced by existing stereotypes that may be attached to certain accents, physical features, or places of residence or education. Lambert et al. (1960) examined this phenomenon specifically as it applied to language stereotypes. Using a "matched guise" technique (with bilingual speakers reading the same message in two languages, subjects questioned on their impressions of the speakers without knowing that the same individuals appeared in two guises), the authors found that evaluations of personality characteristics of the speakers reflected the prevailing majority/minority group stereotypes. Thus both English speaking and French speaking Canadians evaluated the English guises more favorably than the French guises, and the French speaking subjects evaluated the French guises significantly less favorably than did the English speakers. This was interpreted as evidence for a minority group reaction on the part of the French sample.

Although related, the questions we raise in this study do not focus on the effects of language use on personality perception, but rather on the relation-ship between perceived language skill (specifically interpreting) and perceived cultural background, and the relationship between subjective and objec-tive assessments. It is of interest whether raters' perceptions of the interpreters appear to be influenced by personal characteristics unrelated to competence, and whether different raters tend to like the same interpreters. Also there is a persistent informal claim among fluent signers (both deaf and hearing) that they can identify the hearing status of other signers, and of their parents, by the way they sign. It is not clear exactly what signals are supposed to reveal this infermation to the observer, but part of the claim is subject to scrutiny from the data reported in this study—at least with regard to the hearing status of the interpreters' parents.

Three formal hypotheses are specifically addressed:
1. Raters will agree with one another in their subjective evaluations of sign language interpreters;
2. Subjective ratings will be positively correlated with objective assessments of accuracy;
3. Subjective raters will be able to determine whether interpreters had deaf or hearing parents.

The experiment

The testing materials consisted of four passages, each approximately two and one-half minutes long and excerpted from the tape-recorded tests of 25 sign language interpreters originally taken in 1973 for a study on interpreter competence (Quigley et al. 1973, Rudser & Strong 1985). Two of the passages were samples of the subjects signing. In one they had been instructed to transliterate (i.e. "sign in English"), in the other they were required to interpret (i.e. use American Sign Language, ASL). The signed passages were copied on half-inch VHS videotapes in four different random orders. The spoken passages were recorded on audio cassettes, also in four different random orders.

Significant changes have occurred in sign language interpreting in the twelve years since these data were collected, particularly in the vocabulary used to describe various interpreting processes. These changes underlie major differences in the understanding of the processes themselves.

Traditionally the terms *interpret* and *translate* were often used synonymously; when a distinction was made, *interpret* referred to speech, and *translate* referred to writing. In the early years of the sign language interpreting discipline, publications reflec-ted very different use of the terms. Youngs, in the first handbook for interpreters, defined interpreting as "an explanation of another person's remarks through the language of signs, informal gesture, or pantomime" (1965: 6); and translating as a "verbatim presentation of another person's remarks through the language of signs and fingerspelling" (1965: 7). Sign language to English change was referred to as "reverse translating" and "reverse interpreting." Rudser (1978) discussed the difficulties with these early terms and definitions, and more recently, new terminology has come into general use. In the current RID Handbook (Caccamise 1980), for example, interpreting is described as operating (in either direction) between American Sign Language and spoken English, and "transliterating" (replacing the term "translating") as operating between Manually Coded English and spoken English.

Procedures

Twelve subjects took part in this study, six of them were deaf and six hearing. The deaf subjects rated the signed passages, and the hearing subjects rated the spoken passages. The deaf raters watched the interpreted excerpts on a 25-inch television monitor (fed by a JVC portable VHS playback deck), seeing the interpreters in one of the four different random orders. The study was introduced to them as an experiment to find out the opinions of subjective judges concerning the performances of a group of sign language interpreters. Subjects were told they would see each interpreter performing two short parts of two interpreting tasks, in one of which the interpreter would be likely to use ASL. They were asked to watch the excerpts and fill out a short evaluation form (See Appendix 1), indicating whether they liked the interpreter, the level of signing ability, the degree to which he or she was easy to follow and pleasurable to watch, whether his or her parents may have been deaf, and whether more English-like or ASL-like signing was used. Additional comments were invited at the bottom of the form. Raters were not given the original texts of the passages and were asked not to take into account how accurate they imagined the interpreter to be. They could fill out the rating sheet as they watched, or after pausing the tape. The task required about 90 minutes to complete and the subjects were each paid twenty dollars.

The hearing raters were given a small portable audiotape recorder (Panasonic RQ337) with a set of lightweight headphones and a tape with the spoken excerpts in one of four random orders. The study was introduced to them as an experiment to find out the opinions of subjective judges in evaluating the spoken output of sign language interpreters. They were told that they would hear two short voicing episodes for each interpreter, but were not told that in one case the signer had used ASL and in the other, English. They were asked to listen to the excerpts and fill out the relevant forced-choice evaluation form (Appendix 2) indicating whether they found the interpreter jerky or fluent, unpleasant or pleasant to listen to, difficult or easy to understand, and an overall like or dislike. In addition they were asked to indicate whether the interpreter did better on the first or second passage and may have had deaf parents. Additional remarks were invited. As with the deaf raters, the hearing subjects had no access to the original texts and were asked to ignore the level of accuracy they imagined the interpreter to attain. This task also required about 90 minutes and the subjects were paid twenty dollars each.

Each evaluation sheet was checked for completeness and the rater asked to fill in any missing items. A total score of 21 points was possible, 15 for the three multiple choice scales (scored $1 - 5$), and 6 on the overall rating (e.g. 6 for "like," O for "dislike"). The minimum possible score was three.

The deaf subjects were all adults, three male and three female, and all prelingually deaf. All had some college education and while better qualified educationally than most deaf individuals were suited to the subject matter of the interpreted extracts. All six were fluent signers. Three (of hearing parents) had been educated primarily in oral programs; the other three (two of deaf parents) had attended residential schools that were not considered oral. The study was described to them in sign by a sign language interpreter with excellent skills in both ASL and English.

The six hearing subjects, five females and one male, were also college educated. Three had had regular experience communicating with deaf people and were skilled signers, while the others had had no previous contact with deaf people. They were given directions by the same interpreter, using normal spoken English. None of the hearing subjects had deaf parents. The 12 subjects were between 22 and 39 years old.

Recorded excerpts from 25 interpreters, 12 male and 13 female, were used in this study. Ten of them had hearing parents and the other 15 (5 male, 10 female) had deaf parents. Their range in age was from 25 to 56. They had originally been chosen to represent a range of abilities; a subsequent analysis of their test performances confirmed this. The ten highest scores and the two lowest were given to interpreters in the group with deaf parents. Those in the hearing-parent group ranked in the lower middle part of the distribution.

Agreement of subjective raters

The relationships among the ratings made by the deaf subjects were found to correlate well for each pair (Table 1), with Pearson r coefficients from 0.54 to 0.86. High correlations were also found for the hearing raters (Table 2), with a range from 0.52 to 0.86. Furthermore, a comparison between the deaf and hearing raters shows quite high levels of agreement (Table 3), although one would not expect subjective ratings of signing and voicing by different judges to be comparable. These high correlations are almost certainly partly due to the wide spread of abilities among the interpreters, a spread plainly evident in the samples used for rating. Although raters were instructed not to take perceived accuracy into account, the interpreters' varied abilities apparently influenced their interpreting styles and thus probably the ratings they received.

Table 1. Pearson r correlation coefficients: deaf raters' judgments of   interpreters' signing.

	R 2	R 3	R 4	R 5	R 6
R 1	0.86	0.75	0.71	0.70	0.62
R 2		0.66	0.70	0.73	0.70
R 3			0.66	0.61	0.56
R 4				0.73	0.63
R 5					0.54

Table 2. Correlation coefficients: hearing raters' judgments of interpreters' spoken performance.

	R 8	R 9	R 10	R 11	R 12
R 7	0.54	0.64	0.68	0.82	0.83
R 8		0.69	0.52	0.61	0.58
R 9			0.70	0.66	0.78
R 10				0.69	0.70
R 11					0.86

Table 3. Correlation coefficients: hearing & deaf raters' judgmentof interpreters' voicing & signing.

	R 1	R 2	R 3	R 4	R 5	R 6
R 7	0.46	0.54	0.53	0.57	0.52	0.51
R 8	0.49	0.45	0.58	0.53	0.44	0.50
R 9	0.33	0.31	0.46	0.63	0.30	0.33
R 10	0.59	0.54	0.67	0.69	0.57	0.40
R 11	0.47	0.49	0.61	0.57	0.51	0.55
R 12	0.38	0.40	0.42	0.60	0.42	0.49

Subjective vs. objective ratings

To test whether subjective ratings objective ratings. related to objective measures, the raters' scores were compared with accuracy scores by using the Strong and Rudser (1985) instrument for the assessment of sign language interpreters. Two scores were used for this purpose, a combined score on signing tasks and a combined score on the voicing tasks. Correlations between the subjective ratings of the deaf judges and signing accuracy of the interpreters ranged from 0.63 to 0.70 (Table 4). Between scores of the hearing judges and voicing accuracy scores the correlations ranged from 0.59 to 0.79 (Table 5). These consistently high correlations further indicate potentially strong effects of the interpreters' basic abilities on how positively they are perceived by judges who have no objective data for judging the accuracy of the interpretations they are witnessing.

Table 4. Correlation coefficients: deaf raters' judgments w/ signing accuracy scores. (All values significant at p ≤ 0.001,1-tailed).

Rater	R 1	R 2	R 3	R 4	R 5	R 6
Score	0.64	0.70	0.68	0.63	0.64	0.64

Table 5. Correlation coefficients for hearing raters' judgments of interpreters' voicing with voicing accuracy scores (All values significant at p ≤ 0.001, 1-tailed).

Rater	R 7	R 8	R 9	R 10	R 11	R 12
Score	0.79	0.63	0.72	0.59	0.79	0.76

These findings might be taken as evidence supporting the use of more subjective methods of assessing sign language interpreters. However, such conclusions would be shortsighted for two reasons. First, although the correlations are high enough to reach statistical significance at the one one–thousandth level of probability, no coefficient was higher than 0.79, which implies rank orders considerably at variance from those arising from the objective evaluations.

Furthermore, although inter-rater reliability was high, the average quotient (0.52 to 0.86) was far lower than that achieved among the objective raters (0.93 to 0.99; Strong & Rudser 1985)—lower indeed than would be required of any instrument used for rating job applicants or examinees for a professional license. Thus a measure relying on subjective ratings alone, even with good reliability, would almost certainly mis-classify quite a large percentage of whatever sample was being rated.

Deaf or hearing parents?

Ten of the 25 interpreters were from hearing families; 15 had deaf parents. In most cases, the number of judges' correct guesses was no greater than one would expect from chance. Among the deaf raters, of the 90 guesses (= No. judges X No. interpreters), 55 were incorrect. The same interpreters were consistently misidentified (4 from the deaf-parent group were wrongly assigned to the other group by all 6 judges), although all but two obtained at least one false nomination. However, the deaf judges were more successful at identifying members of the hearing-parent group, making only 7 errors out of 60 (see Table 6). The guesses of the hearing judges approximated chance for both hearing-parent (27 out of 60) and deaf-parent groups (42 out of 90), with at least one wrong identification going to all but one of the interpreters.

Table 6. Number of **incorrect** guesses as to parental hearing
status of interpreters.

Judge status:	Interpr w/ HP	Interpr. w/ DP
Deaf	7/60	55/90
Hearing	27/60	42/90

It would appear from these data that the hearing status of a signer's parents is only likely to be identifiable with any consistency if the parents were hearing. It is apparently impossible to make such an identification from samples of spoken interpreting. One may make some speculations as to

the kind of information the raters used in arriving at their
decisions on interpreters' parents' hearing status by looking
at which interpreters they assigned to which group, and at
their comments. By far the most common strategy among the
deaf raters seemed to be to assign the interpreter to the deaf-
parent group if they liked him or her (and they tended to like
them the more accurate they were), and to the hearing-parent
group if they did not. This explains some of the
misidentifications among the deaf-parent group (i.e. some of
the poorest performers had deaf parents); also the successful
identifications among the hearing-parent group, most of
whom were in the moderate to low end of the rankings. One
rater, however, from an oral background and with hearing
parents, went against the trend by identifying the most liked
interpreters as having hearing parents, thus contributing to
the number of erroneous guesses, because the most skilled
interpreters in this sample indeed had deaf parents. A second
discernible strategy involved the judgment of use of ASL or
English. Five of the six deaf raters tended to assign
interpreters to the deaf-parent group if they also rated them as
using more ASL than English, particularly if they liked them
overall. They correspondingly identified the interpreters they
liked least as using mostly English. There were more
exceptions to this rule than for that linking liking and deaf
parents.

One of the deaf raters seemed to associate degree of
expressiveness with having deaf parents. In many cases this
rater added comments such as "very expressive," "signing
lacked expression," or "no facial expression, body too stiff."
Without exception this rater identified the more expressive
signers as having deaf parents. Among the hearing raters,
perceived quality also appeared to be the main deciding
factor. For four of the hearing raters the most liked
interpreters were assigned deaf parentage, but for the other
two the high scoring interpreters were assigned hearing
parentage. One hearing rater (who had worked in the field of
deafness for several years) frequently used age as a criterion,
feeling—often correctly—that the older sounding speakers
probably had deaf parents. However, overall skill seemed to
be the most crucial factor for this rater, whose top selections

were all assigned deaf parents and whose least favored were assumed to have hearing parents. It should be noted that the best interpreters today are less likely all to be from deaf families than they were when the data used in this study were originally collected. The strategy that was apparently successful in identifying interpreters from hearing families is unlikely to work as well under current conditions.

Conclusions

From this study of a small sample of hearing and deaf raters of sign language interpreters some tentative conclusions can be drawn and implications considered for future research. First, judges tend to like and dislike the same interpreters, regardless of their own background (but given a higher than average education and a somewhat narrow age range). This may be partly attributable to the wide range of abilities among the sample of interpreters observed and needs to be further examined with interpreters of more comparable skills.

Second, subjective judgments tend to correlate with objective measures of accuracy in interpreting, again with the proviso that wide-ranging abilities might have been partly responsible for this finding. Nonetheless, these correlations were not perfect, and inter-judge agreement was not nearly as high as that found among raters using an objective instrument. This suggests that while subjective ratings provide an interesting and useful dimension of interpreter assessment, they should not replace a sound objective measure. This finding has implications for the evaluation procedure of the Registry of Interpreters for the Deaf, which is essentially subjective, although the questions are phrased in the form "Did the interpreter do _____?" or "Did the interpreter use _____?" rather than "Did you like the interpreter?" The RID uses three raters to evaluate each interpreter and averages their scores. No inter–rater reliability figures are published, but if they are not consistently above the 0.90 mark, this could lead to vulnerability in issues of discrimination under Title VII of the 1964 Civil Rights Act. Such problems might be avoided if a demonstrably objective dimension were added to the evaluation procedure, such as that proposed by Strong and Rudser (1985).

Third, deaf raters were not successful in identifying which interpreters had deaf parents by the way they signed, although they correctly identified those with hearing parents 88 percent of the time. This would suggest that the primary criterion for identifying a signer with deaf parents is the quality of the signing. A study using signers of equivalent ability might reveal secondary criteria that are obscured when the range of skill is great as in the sample described

Note: This study was made possible in part by Grant G 008 300 146 from the National Institute for Handi-capped Research to the University of California, San Francisco, RT23 Center on Deafness. Some of the original data were collected by Stephen Quigley, Barbara Brasel, and Dale Montanelli under the support of Grant SRS 14P 55400/5 from the Division of Research and Demonstration Grants, Social & Rehabilitation Service, Department of Health, Education & Welfare, Washington, DC 20201. The authors thank these original investigators for making their data available for our analysis. Thanks also to the 25 interpreters who allowed us to question them all these years later and who provided us with valuable information about their backgrounds. Finally, thanks for the valuable advice and support from Mimi Lou both as friend and scholar and in her capacity as Director of Research at the Center on Deafness.

Appendix 1

Interpreter Rating Form: Sign Language

Circle one choice on each line
(Low SL ability) 1 2 3 4 5 (High SL ability)
(Hard to follow) 1 2 3 4 5 (Easy to follow)
(Unpleasant to 1 2 3 4 5 (Pleasant to watch)

Overall evaluation   Dislike   O.K.   Like

This interpreter uses more   English   ASL

This interpreter's parents were   Hearing   Deaf

Comments:

REFERENCES

Caccamise, F.
    1980   *Introduction to Interpreting*. Silver Spring,
           MD: Registry of Interpreters for the Deaf.

Lambert, W. et al.
    1960   Evaluational reactions to spoken language,
    Journal of Abnormal & Social Psychology   10, 44-51.
Quigley, S., B. Brasel & D. Montanelli
    1973   Interpreters for Deaf People: Selection,
    evaluation & classification. Final Report
    HEW SRS 14-P-55400/5.

Rudser, S.
　　1978   Interpreting: Difficulties in present termin-
　　　　　　ology, *Interpreter News*.
　　——— & M. Strong
　　[1985   An examination of some personal
　　　　　　characteristics & abilities of sign language
　　interpreters.Unpublished MS, Center on
　　Deafness, UCSF.]
Strong, M. & S. Rudser
　　1985   An assessment instrument for sign
　　　　　　language interpreters. *Sign Language
　　Studies* 49, 344-362.
Youngs, J.
　　1965   Introduction: Interpreting for deaf persons.
　　　　　　In *Interpreting for Deaf People*. Washington,
　　DC: U.S.Dept. of Health, Education &
　　Welfare.

II. An Examination of Some Personal Characteristics & Abilities of Sign Language Interpreters

Steven Fritsch Rudser
Michael Strong

Abstract

Very little research has focused on those characteristics of sign language interpreters predictive of high levels of skill in interpreting. This study analyzes data collected some 13 years ago by Quigley et al. (1974) on 25 interpreters who were given interpreting tasks to perform and were measured on a number of personal variables. Using a specially designed objective instrument for the evaluation of interpreting abilities the present authors found that most of the predictor variables hypothesized in the earlier study as related to interpreting skills were indeed poor predictors. Multiple regression analysis revealed the importance of certain personality traits which differed according to whether the interpreters came from hearing or deaf families. These data provide a basis for comparison with contemporary interpreters in order to document the nature and extent of the changes that are apparently widespread throughout this profession. Further research is called for to examine carefully practicing interpreters and to take into account variables that were not considered when these data were originally collected.

The interpreting scene

The need for sign language interpreters has increased dramatically in recent years. A generally heightened awareness of the rights of deaf persons has meant that more interpreters are called for in legal, medical, entertainment, higher educational, social, psychological, and religious settings and the passage of Public Law 94-142 has created mainstream programs for hearing-impaired children, thereby extending the demand for interpreters to primary and secondary schools as well. Whereas 20 years ago very few people attempted to make a living as sign language interpreters, today there are several thousand who derive at least a portion of their income from sign language interpreting (source: Registry of Interpreters for the Deaf, Silver Spring, MD 20910). These interpreters acquire their skills at any of a number of interpreter training programs across the country, which have been established since the early seventies. A large proportion of these programs are to be found in two-year community colleges, however, and it is clear that more time than they provide is needed to develop sophisticated interpreting skills (Rudser, in press). Spoken language interpreters, for example, undergo much longer training and are required to have high levels of fluency in the relevant languages before beginning their training programs.

The increased demand for interpreters and for more effective and extended training programs is accompanied by a need to know more about what qualities are required of a good interpreter and the best means of assessing these qualities. Unfortu-nately, almost no research has been done to determine the characteristics that are predictive of good sign language interpreters, and very little choice still exists in methods of evaluation. This situation is partly explained by the relative youthfulness of the profession, the problems inherent in assessing interpreter competence, and the lack of funding available for research on sign language interpreting. Improvements in the system of evaluating and selecting interpreter trainees would help to counteract some of the problems that have arisen from minimal training programs and the resulting need to hire interpreters who often are not fully qualified to do the work.

In one study, Schein examined the personality characteristics of working sign language interpreters and found, using the Edwards Personality Prefer-ence Scale (EPPS), that the more skilled interpreter could be described as one who: "desires to be the center of attention and to be independent, and is not rigid" (1974: 42). Schein himself cautioned against over-interpretation of his findings, noting his small sample size (20 subjects), a subjective rating system that produced low inter-rater reliability, and the limitations of examining already practicing interpreters rather than testing trainees once during training and again when they had attained their maximal level of interpreting skills.

Quigley, Brasel, and Montanelli (1973) began a study to examine the characteristics of sign language interpreters with a view to determining whether there were commonalties among the traits of those displaying similar levels of interpreting ability. They were unable to complete the study for lack of continued funding. They did, however, collect data on 30 subjects, and these materials were recently made available to the present authors for analysis in a current series of investigations of sign language interpreter competence. This paper reports on the results of one part of the analysis, the aim of which was to isolate those factors that are predictive of sign language interpreting abilities.

Fifteen females and fifteen males were chosen for the original study (Quigley et al. 1973) on the basis of recommendations by project staff or advisory board members, and their sign language skills were roughly precategorized according to a five-point scale ranging from minimal (1) to fluent (5). The thirty were equally distributed across this continuum, although subjects functioning at the lower levels were reportedly harder to find. They ranged in age from 23 to 56. Data on 25 of these subjects were usable in the analysis reported here.

The 30 original subjects were brought to the University of Illinois and given a series of interpreting tasks to perform, as well as a number of psychological tests. The first of the interpreting tasks involved a taped lecture, which was to be "translated" (transliterated from spoken English to manual English). The second was an audiotaped lecture and story to "interpret" from spoken English to a more ASL-like form of signing (see pp. ?? above). The rate of speech in the stimulus material ranged from 130 to 190 words per minute, with the speeds increasing incrementally to the upper limit, after which the speaker used a normal pace for the last segment of the passage. The subjects' signed output was in turn video recorded, using black and white Sony reel-to-reel equipment. Recordings were made in a studio, with subjects wearing plain blue sweaters in front of a plain curtain and framed from just below the waist to just above the head. In addition, several stories were signed by deaf people (half in a signed form of English and half in a form that ranged between

Pidgin Sign English (PSE) and ASL; the subjects voiced these while being recorded on audiotape. The materials chosen for the tasks were considered by the researchers to be of the type that most interpreters were likely to have experienced.

The psychological tests administered to each subject focused on four major areas that the original investigators had identified as potentially related to interpreting skill; these were: cognitive abilities, perceptual abilities, psychomotor abilities, and affective characteristics.

To measure cognitive abilities the following standardized tests were used: the Wechsler Adult Intelligence Scale (WAIS), which gives an intelli-gence quotient (IQ), the Modern Language Aptitude Test (MLAT), which measures auditory memory and information processing, and the Christensen–Guilford Fluency Tests, which measure word, ideational, associational, and expressive fluency. Perceptual abilities were measured by the Minnesota Paper Form Board, which tests ability to visualize and manipulate objects in space, and the Memory for Designs Test, which measures perceptual–motor coordination based on immediate memory. Psychomotor abilities were assessed using the Purdue Pegboard, which tests manual dexterity on both gross and fine motor skills, and the Embedded Figures Test, which measures the ability to look at complex configu-rations and to respond to parts. Affective factors, i.e. personality traits, were measured by the California Personality Inventory (CPI).

In addition, a personal and family history questionnaire was administered to obtain infor-mation on the professional, academic, and family backgrounds of the subjects. This information was subsequently lost, but 25 of the original 30 subjects were successfully located and interviewed 12 years later in order to retrieve that part of the information whose accuracy was not affected by the passage of time. These 25 subjects provide the data for the analysis presented here.

Research question

The aim of this study was to find out which cognitive, perceptual, psychomotor, and affective characteristics are associated with sign language interpreting abilities. Secondary goals were to construct and pilot test an instrument for evaluating interpreter accuracy, and to use the data as pilot material in the development of a similar, contemporary study of sign language interpreters.

The first major task in the analysis was to assess the interpreting samples for each subject. For this a measurement instrument was developed (see Strong & Rudser 1985), which enabled the signed and spoken output to be rated objectively for accuracy. By taking samples from the interpreted output, breaking them down into individual propositions, and then comparing each proposition with the original stimulus, it was possible to arrive at a largely objective measure of accuracy with a high inter-rater reliability (0.93 to 0.99 on overall scores for each subject). Separate accuracy scores were obtained for signing translating and signing interpreting, voicing transliterating and voicing interpreting. This instrument also provided information on the use of fingerspelling and the ability to read it, the degree to which the interpreter made cultural adjustments, and the proportion of ASL use to English. In addition, a subjective rating system was developed, whereby a small selection of deaf and hearing persons evaluated a sample of the signed and spoken interpretations according to their personal preferences, but without reference to degree of accuracy (see the preceding article).

Pearson product–moment correlation coefficients were calculated to assess the relationships that pertained between the predictor and outcome variables, and among the different outcome variables. The sub-scale scores on the CPI were subjected to a stepwise multiple regression analysis with the combined accuracy scores for the various interpreting, transliterating, and voicing tasks. Relationships were examined among all 25 subjects and also separately for the 10 with hearing parents and 15 with deaf parents; for it was felt that there might well be basic differences between members of the two groups in the motivation to become an interpreter and in the circumstances surrounding their advent to the profession. This might conceivably mean that subjects in the hearing-parent group would have different distributions of the variables under consideration from those in the deaf-parent group.

Results & discussion

1. Relationships: scores on different interpreting tasks

The first finding of note with regard to the interpreters' performance on the signing and voicing tasks is that the deaf-parent group and the hearing-parent group indeed showed different distributions of interpreting skills. The top performers overall were all from the deaf-parent group, as were the two lowest scorers; and those from the hearing-parent group ranked in the lower middle part of the distribution. These unequal distributions have implications for other findings in the study. Not only are the interpreters with deaf parents disproportionately represented among the better performers, but the range of scores among members of that group is much greater (Table 1). These two factors have the potential for exaggerating correlation between predictor and outcome variables for the deaf-parent group, while minimizing the size of the correlation for the hearing-parent group. The same factors also support the decision to look at the results for the two groups separately as well as for the sample as a whole.

In general, scores on the different voicing and signing tasks correlated significantly with one another (Table 2). For example, subjects who performed well on the signing transliterating (ST) ask were likely to get good scores for signing-interpreting (SI) and on the two voicing tests (VT & VI). One exception to this was that SI accuracy did not correlate significantly with VI accuracy. This could have occurred if the voicing interpreting task (or the sample section selected for analysis) was comparatively less complicated than the other tasks and therefore had allowed the less skilled subjects to get higher scores, while those with superior ability had less room for improvement, thus minimizing the differences that the more difficult tasks revealed.

Table 1. Descriptive statistics for objective scores on interpreting tasks.

Subjects:		Mean	SD	Range
All	STI	424.4	76.4	302
N = 25	VTI	468.8	99.5	376
	SVTI	893.2	153.3	525
With		Mean	SD	Range
hearing	STI	373.2	75.1	259
parents	VTI	434.6	53.1	194
N = 10	SVTI	807.8	92.3	264
With		Mean	SD	Range
deaf	STI	458.5	57.0	153
parents	VTI	491.7	117.4	376
N = 15	SVTI	950.1	161.7	525

Key: STI = Combined scores signing tasks
            VTI = Combined scores voicing tasks
            STVI = Combined scores on both tasks

Table 2. Correlation coefficients for objective scores on interpreting tasks.

All Subjects, N = 25

	SIF	STF	VF	VI	VT	SI
ST	0.30	0.49*	-0.53*	0.48*	0.57*	0.73*
SI	-0.11	0.41*	-0.41*	-0.27	0.42	
VT	0.04	0.49*	-0.95*	0.76*		
VI	0.07	-0.27	-0.75			
VF	-0.08	-0.55				
STF	0.22					

Subjects with Hearing Parents, N = 10

	SIF	STF	VF	VI	VT	SI
ST	-0.61	0.26	0.00	-0.28	0.06	0.61
SI	-0.11	0.33	-0.13*	-0.22	0.39	
VT	0.24	0.67*	-0.83*	0.15		
VI	0.05	-0.47	-0.27			
VF	-0.18	-0.65*				
STF	0.27					

Subjects with Deaf Parents, N = 15

	SIF	STF	VF	VI	VT	SI
ST	-0.02	0.63*	-0.72*	0.79*	0.75*	0.76*
SI	0.01	0.49	-0.48	0.46	0.42	
VT	0.03	0.44	-0.97*	0.89*		
VI	0.14	0.56*	-0.85*			
VF	-0.10	-0.49				
STF	0.23					

* = $p \leq 0.5$

Key: ST = Signing Transliterating Accuracy
SI = Signing Interpreting Accuracy
VT = Voiclng Transliterating Accuracy
VI = Voicing Interpreting Accuracy
VF = Voicing Flngerspelling Errors
STF = Signing Transliterating Flngerspelling Use
SIF = Signing Interpreting Fingerspelling Use

A finding of potential interest concerns the fingerspelling scores. For the voicing tasks, the fingerspelling score (VF) refers to errors made in reading words that were fingerspelled on the stimulus tape. As can be seen in Table 1, significant negative correlation resulted between these scores and scores on all other tasks. This would suggest that skill at reading fingerspelling is predictive of interpreting ability in general and thus might provide a simple testing procedure that could be used for evaluating and screening interpreters, interpreter trainees, and students. Degree of fingerspelling use while transliterating (STF) also correlated significantly with the scores for interpreting and transliterating accuracy, suggesting that the more skilled interpreters are able to use more fingerspelling when transliterating. Such a skill is used less when interpreting, and this is reflected in the non-significant correlation for fingerspelling on the interpreting tasks with other accuracy scores. Use of fingerspelling while interpreting correlated negatively with ASL use, suggesting either that raters associated ASL with signing that included less fingerspelling or that those subjects whose signing was closer to ASL tended to fingerspell less frequently.

While most of the associations pertaining to the group as a whole held for the subgroup with deaf parents, when considered separately, they did not for the subgroup of subjects with hearing parents. This may in part be a function of the difference in sample size and range of scores between the two subgroups (see Table 1). It may also be true that the skills of individuals in the hearing-parent group were more uneven.

2. Relationships: interpreting accuracy & predictor variables.

No significant correlation were recorded between interpreting accuracy and: IQ, field dependence, manual dexterity, memory, spatial aptitude, verbal fluency, or language aptitude. For IQ the lack of association is corroborated by Schein (1976). The IQ scores of the subjects in this study, as in Schein's, were generally higher and showed less variance than the average, ranging from 99 to 136 for Verbal IQ and 95 to 140 for Performance IQ. It is possible that the lack of association between interpreting skills and any of these variables is partly a result of a sample that was selected without controlling for degree of experience and number of years interpreting, and of whom many were not trained interpreters. Clearly, some of the subjects had not yet reached the upper limits of their potential, while others who had been signing for many years were not primarily interpreters and had not had any formal training in the profession. Thus it cannot be maintained that the findings reported here would apply to the trained professional interpreters of today.

Furthermore, some of the variables might have been better assessed using different tests of the sort of memory capabilities needed for interpreting work rather than the Memory for Designs Test. Manual dexterity measured by the Purdue Pegboard, typically used to assess motor skills for some kinds of assembly work, is probably an inappropriate test of the skills needed in sign language interpreting. Nevertheless, these results suggest that the characteristics under investigation are not the most critical for predicting interpreting abilities, and that other factors are apparently playing a more important role.

Use of fingerspelling while interpreting correlated negatively with verbal fluency. Since this test measures the ability to think of synonyms and alternative expressions that fit a given sentential format, it is logical that those who score high on verbal fluency would less often need to resort to fingerspelling when interpreting.

For the hearing-parent group, number of years signing correlated negatively with transliterating accuracy. This a puzzling finding; it may be only partially explained by the fact that the number of years since the subject first learned to sign does not necessarily reflect the degree and intensity of signing experience, or the number of years working as an interpreter. In other words, subjects in this group probably include "pseudo interpreters" (e.g. teachers and parents of deaf children), who worked less often, if at all, as formal interpreters and focused less on absolute accuracy in their signing than did subjects who had learned to sign more recently but principally for interpreting purposes—where accuracy is more salient than in other situations. However, the number of years signing did correlate positively with

voicing skills and negatively with errors in reading
fingerspelling, suggesting that receptive abilities may be
more a function of long use and practice than are productive
signing skills.

A stepwise multiple regression analysis of the California
Personality Inventory subscales with combined outcome
variables indicated that certain personality traits appear to
play a role in distinguishing good interpreters. Table 3 lists
the traits that contributed to the variance of combined tasks
scores for all subjects, and for both parentage subgroups (F
to enter =1, F to remove = 1, tolerance = 0.001).

Table 3. Summary of stepwise multiple regression analyses on
personality traits and combined interpreting tasks.

All Subjects N=25		Subjects w/deaf par. N=15	
Trait	R^2	Trait	R^2
- Good impression	8	+ Commonalty	17
+ Capacity for status	12	+ Social presence	42
		+ Achieve via indep.	49
Subjects w/ hrg par. N=10		- IQ efficiency	61
- Responsibility	71	- Good impression	65
+ Flexibility	84	+ Responsibility	69
- Good impression	95	+ Sociability	80

This Table allows a cautious profiling good interpreters
among the deaf-parent group as follows (Descriptors are in
decreasing order of importance and together explain 80% of
the variance):
"dependable, tactful, patient and conscientious"
(+Commonalty)
"active, insightful and with an expressive nature" (+Social
Presence)
"mature, dominant, self-reliant and with superior judgment"
(+Achievement via Independence)
"conventional and stereotyped in thinking, easygoing,
defensive" (-Intellectual Efficiency)
"self-centered, aloof, and unconcerned with how others react
to them" (-Good Impression)
"dignified, independent, dependable, conscientious,
efficient" (+Responsibility)

"outgoing, competitive, original and fluent in thought" (+Sociability).

For those interpreters with hearing parents, the profile is somewhat different. Ninety-five percent of the variance on the competence measures is explained by the presence of the following (also in decreasing order):

"somewhat changeable, under controlled, impulsive and temperamental" (-Responsibility)

"cognitively and socially flexible and adaptable, insightful, assertive and egoistic" (+Flexibility)

"self-centered, aloof, and unconcerned with how others react to them" (-Good Impression).

Not altogether surprisingly, this is a considerably different constellation of traits from that found among the deaf-parent group, and neither group shares all the characteristics found by Schein (1974). It should be remembered, however, that these were interpreters practicing more than 12 years ago, and because conditions have changed so much in the intervening years, it is likely that interpreters who come to the profession today are rather different from those who were involved in the original study. In fact, from the follow-up background information on the subjects, it was found that only two of the ten subjects in this group still identify themselves as interpreters, while some of the others continue to be involved with deafness as educators or parents; still others no longer have any connection with the field.

When all subjects are considered as a single group, 12% of the variance is explained by the following characteristics:

"self centered, aloof, and unconcerned with how others react to them" (-Good Impression),

"ambitious, active, self-seeking, effective in communication, having personal scope and breadth of interests" (+Capacity for Status).

These findings should be interpreted with some caution for two reasons. First, the number of subjects in each subgroup is smaller than desirable for regression analyses with this many varieties, and the skill levels were not similarly distributed among members of each group. Second, while the traits in the CPI have been validated in a series of different studies, correlation coefficients tended to be moderately low (all below 0.50 according to the official manual). Test-retest reliability quotients, however, were satisfactorily high for the samples published in the manual.

Conclusion

The results of this study appear to indicate that few of the cognitive, perceptual, psychomotor, or affective characteristics chosen by Quigley et al. (1973) are significant predictors of sign language interpreting accuracy, as represented by practitioners in the early 1970s. While certain constellations of personality traits suggest associations with interpreting skills, limitations of sample size (particularly of the hearing and deaf parent subgroups) demand a cautious interpretation of the findings. Also the subjects were not controlled for interpreting experience, thus allowing the inclusion of some interpreters in the study who had not yet reached their optimum levels of performance and others who were not trained interpreters at all; hence introducing error into the analysis.

Furthermore, the conditions for sign language interpreters have changed considerably since these data were collected, as reflected in the greater diversity of individuals attracted to the field, improvements in job status and working conditions, a broadening of settings in which interpreters are required, the creation of formal training programs, and considerable increase in both the demands on interpreters and the standards required of them. It is possible, for example, that many of the interpreters who were working in 1973 were not really interpreters as they would be defined today. Such changes suggest that more research is needed on interpreters currently practicing their profession in order to establish what constellation of personal traits and abilities is predictive of sign language interpreting skill as related to present conditions. It is only with the benefit of such data as were analyzed in this study, however, that the effects of such changes said to be taking place among interpreters for the deaf can be documented and close comparisons made with the characteristics of contemporary practitioners. It may be found that some of the characteristics that were not predictive of the interpreters in this study indeed discriminate between the better and worse performers of today. Alternatively, there may be other factors, such as general knowledge, short term verbal memory, and vocabulary breadth, that were not tested by the investigators in 1973 but that are predictive of successful sign language interpreting. Current research by the present authors will attempt to answer these questions.

Meanwhile we have learned from these initial data that the various sub-skills of interpreting are indeed related, with fingerspelling ability being a very good indicator of transliterating skills in general; also that good interpreters appear to have certain personality traits in common. If these findings are replicated in future studies of interpreters working today, these and any other predictors that are discovered could facilitate selection processes and to some extent improve training procedures as well as serve ultimately to raise standards within the profession.

REFERENCES

Caccamise, F.
    1980   *Introduction to Interpreting.* Silver Spring
    MD: Registry of Interpreters for the Deaf. Quigley S., B.
Brasel & D. Montanelli
    1973   *Interpreters for Deaf People.* Final Report
    HEW SRS 14-P-55400/5.
Rudser, S5.
    1978   Interpreting: Difficulties in present terminology,
    Interpreter News. i.p. Special issues in present terminology.
    In *Language Learning & Deafness*, Strong ed. Cambridge:
    Cambridge Univ. Press.
Strong M. & S. Rudser
    1985   An assessment instrument for SL
    interpreters, *Sign Language Studies* 49,   344-362.
Youngs J.
    1965   Introduction: Interpreting for deaf persons.
    In *Interpreting for Deaf People.* Washington
    DC: U.S. Department of Health Education & Welfare.

III. LINGUISTIC ANALYSIS OF CHANGES IN INTERPRETERS' LANGUAGE 1973–1985

Steven Fritsch Rudser

Abstract

Two sign language interpreters were recorded as they interpreted and transliterated two spoken English texts in 1973 as part of an investigation of interpreter competence. They were then recorded again interpreting the same material in 1985. The earlier and later interpretations of each are here compared, and the degree to which they use American Sign Language estimated.

Introduction

The formation of the Registry of Interpreters for the Deaf (RID) in 1964 marks the formal beginning of the movement to professionalize sign language intepreting in the United States. During the first decade of this movement many state and local chapters of the RID were formed, a book on the interpreting field was published (Youngs 1965), a national certification program was established (Caccamise et al. 1980), and interpreter training programs were instituted in a number of community colleges. While the first decade emphasized organizational and institutional develoment, the second decade, from 1974 to 1984, can be characterized by conceptual development of the understanding of the role and functions of sign language interpreters. This second decade witnessed the proliferation of research proving that American Sign Language (ASL) is a language, and the publication of books and journals on the topic of interpreting.

Many believe that understanding of the interpreting task has changed very significantly during this period. This belief is supported by a comparison of interpreting and transliterating as they are defined in *Interpreting for Deaf People* (Youngs 1965) and *Introduction to Interpreting* (Caccamise et al. 1980). The former defines interpreting as "an explanation of another person's remarks through the language of signs, informal gestures, or pantomime" (1965:6). "Translating" (the task currently referred to as transliterating) is defined by Youngs as verbatim presentation of another person's remarks through the language of signs and fingerspelling" (1965:7). The *Introduction to Interpreting* refers to interpreting as working between ASL and English, and transliterating as working between spoken English and a signed form of English (or non-audible spoken English, in the case of an oral deaf interpreter).

The underlying difference between these definitions is the conception of ASL as a language. Acknowledgement that ASL is a language has had many implications for interpreting. An interesting issue that comes up as a result of this conceptual change is, what were interpreters doing then, and what are they doing now? Or, more precisely, are these changes in the field of sign language interpreting merely semantic, or have they actually changed the way interpreters work?

The Center on Deafness at the University of California, San Francisco has had the fortuitous opportunity to study these questions as a result of undertaking a project focused on the competence of sign language interpreters. This project is based on an earlier research endeavor conducted at the University of Illinois by Stephen P. Quigley and Barbara Babbini Brasel. The Quigley and Brasel project was done in 1973, and it involved videotaping 30 interpreters of varying skill as they interpreted, transliterated, and voiced prerecorded texts. The subjects for their study were roughly classified by skill into five categories, with '5' representing native or native–like fluency in sign language and '1' representing minimal knowledge of sign language. In addition to interpreting, the subjects were tested on a battery of personality and intelligence tests, with the goal of comparing these test scores with their skill in their interpreting performances. (See above, pp. 15)

Videotaping some of the interpreters involved in the original study as they interpreted the same material twelve years later would make it possible to compare and contrast the interpretation, with an emphasis on the differential use of ASL and English. If the interpretations were not significantly different linguistically, it could be assumed that the historical change in the conceptualization of the interpreter's task and of ASL had exerted little effect on these interpreters. If there were significant differences in the linguistic nature of the early and late interpretations, it is possible that those differences would be a direct result of changes in the field.

Comparison

Subjects for the current study were selected according to several criteria. Only participants from the original group with the highest skills (those rated '5') were considered. The interpreters must have continued their involvement in the interpreting field during the intervening twelve years. They had to have demonstrated knowledge of ASL in the first study. Though participants in the original study were evenly divided, half having deaf parents, half not, only those with deaf parents were considered for this study. None of the interpreters with hearing parents had demonstrated enough knowledge of ASL to be included; thus any differences in their performances between the first and second rounds could easily be attributed to better knowledge of the language rather than the influence of historical changes on the expectations of the interpreting task. The final criterion was willingness to be involved in the study.

Two interpreters, each of whom met the above criteria, were chosen to participate in the study. Each was videotaped while again interpreting the two spoken English passages from the original study. The subjects were instructed to transliterate the first selection and to interpret the second into ASL. They were not told of the specific areas of investigation of the present study.

The English texts that the subjects were asked to interpret and transliterate were each about fifteen minutes long. The rate of speech began at approximately 130 words per minute and increased to about 190. The transliterating text is a lecture about the impact of ego on the ability to speak in public. The text for interpreting is a lecture on child language development, in which a story about a small child is embedded. The story comprises about two–thirds of the material, and the lecture the other third. The material in both texts is quite complicated, and the speech rate would be considered very fast.

In this paper I will discuss the results of analysis of the interpreting sections. Characteristics of the transliterated material will be discussed in a future paper. This leaves four segments, each of the interpreters' interpreting tasks from 1973 and each of their interpreting tasks from 1985. I analyzed these four texts for the presence of four ASL features: Classifiers and size and shape specifiers Rhetorical questions Noun–adjective word order Nonmanual negation. This list is not exhaustive or definitive, but these are simply four ASL linguistic structures that stand in contrast to English and are fairly easy to identify and tabulate.

Results

Classifiers:

Subject A used a total of 30 classifiers in 1973. Within this number were seven discrete handshapes. Twenty-one of the 30 classifiers used represented unrepeated combinations of handshapes and movement patterns (e.g. a particular combination that was used only once in the text; nine were repetitions (i.e. a second use of one of the 21 combinations). In 1985 the same interpreter used classifiers a total of 45 times. The number of handshapes increased to ten. Thirty-one of the 45 were unique; 14 were repetitions. Subject B used 22 classifiers in the 1973 study. Five discrete handshapes were used. Thirteen of the 22 classifiers were unrepeated combinations of handshape and movement; 9 were repetitions. In the second round this interpreter used a total of 67 classifiers, with 11 discrete handshapes. Forty-six of the 67 were unrepeated; 21 were repetitions.

Rhetorical questions:

Neither subject used a single rhetorical question in their 1973 interpretations, but both used them fairly frequently in 1985 interpreting. Subject A used a total of 10 rhetorical questions, 6 in the lecture section and 4 in the story section. Subject B used 13, 9 in the lecture and 4 in the story.

Noun–adjective word order:

In the 1973 round there was one instance of noun–adjective word order in Subject A's interpretation, and none in B's. In the 1985 round, Subject A used noun–adjective order 19 times, and B used it 17 times. The single instance of noun–adjective order in 1973 is an interesting exception. Subject A signed the phrase ONE VOICE LESS as an interpretation for the English phrase "one less voice [asking for something]." This is the only time the interpreter placed an adjective after a noun; however, this word order is also acceptable in English.

Nonmanual negation:

There are several facial expressions or movements of the head that signal negation in ASL.

These nonmanual markers can be combined with a sign of negation, but they can also be made simultaneously with another sign or phrase to express negation. In the earlier interpretations neither subject used a nonmanual marker alone to negate a sign or phrase. In the 1985 interpretations Subject B used nonmanual signals for negation 6 times. Subject A did not use any nonmanual signals alone in her 1985 version.

Discussion

For each of the four linguistic features of ASL that were chosen for investigation in this study, there is an increase in use in the later interpretations of the same material. Subject A increased classifier use by 50%, going from no instances of rhetorical questions to 10, and from one instance of noun–adjective order to 19. Although this interpreter did not use nonmanual negation apart from a negative sign, there were numerous instances of changes in the word order so that the negative sign came after the sign or phrase it modified. In addition, Subject A used other nonmanual adjectives and adverbs far more frequently in the second version than in the first.

Subject B actually tripled the number of classifiers in the later round. She went from no rhetorical questions the first time to 13 the second time, and from no instances of noun–adjective word order to 17 in the second version. She did not use nonmanual negation apart from manual signs in the original interpretation but used it 6 times in the second.

One interesting aspect of this study is the

similarity in the number of times in the later version of their interpretations that the subjects used rhetorical questions (10 and 13) and noun–adjective word order (19 and 17). There is some agreement between subjects in the places where these structures are used, but most of the instances do not appear at the same point in the text. The frequency of use of these grammatical structures seems to demonstrate a similarity in interpreting style. Though each of them could have employed either of these structures in more places in the text than they did, greater frequency might have been too repetitive. The subjects seemed to agree on how often it was appropriate to use these two grammatical features.

Both interpreters used rhetorical questions more frequently in the lecture section than in the story section of the text. Sixty per cent of Subject A's and 70% of Subject B's rhetorical questions occurred during the lecture section, although the lecture material accounts for only one third of the total text. By contrast, almost all of the classifiers occurred in the anecdotal or story section; only one of A's 45 classifiers and 2 of B's 67 appeared in the lecture material. The content of the story, because of numerous references to spatial relationships of people and objects, invites the use of classifiers.

It could be assumed that these differences represent changes in only these four linguistic structures. However, preliminary analysis indicates that there are similar increases in the number of instances of other nonmanual markers, inflections on verbs, and topicalization. In addition, for both subjects, mouthing of words decreased drastically in the second version and vocabulary choice was noticeably more varied.

It is clear that there is a significant difference in the amount of ASL used in the 1973 and 1985 interpretations by the same interpreters. Though there are elements of ASL in the 1973 versions, these are primarily associated with sign choice, facial expression, and body shifts. In the later version there is ample evidence of the interpreted text exhibiting ASL features.

In future research, several of the interpreters with hearing parents, who scored highest in the original 1973 study, will be asked to reinterpret this material, to see if similar development can be found in their interpreting. In addition, the transliterated texts of the two subjects described here will be analyzed for ASL and English features, to see if transliterating has gone through any similar changes over the last decade.

REFERENCES

Caccamise F.
  1980 *Introduction to Interpreting.* Silver Spring
        MD: Registry of Interpreters for the Deaf.
Youngs J.
  1965 Introduction: Interpreting for deaf persons.
        In *Interpreting for Deaf People*, Quigley ed.
        Washington DC: US. Department of Health
        Education and Welfare.

Note: This study like the two above was made possible in part through Grant 008 300 146 from the National Institute for Handicapped Research to the University of California San Francisco Center on Deafness. The author would like to thank Mimi WheiPing Lou, Michael Strong, Michael Acree, and James C. Woodward for valuable comments and suggestions. Special thanks also to the two interpreters who took time from extremely busy schedules to assist in this study.

IV. The Effects of Lag Time on Interpreter Errors

Dennis Cokely

Abstract

A popular but naive notion that sign language interpreters should strive for perfect temporal synchrony with the source message has persisted for a long time. This study provides evidence that imposing such a constraint or expectation upon interpreters results in inaccurate interpretation and an increase in interpreter errors or miscues. An analysis and count of miscues in actual interpreter performances has been compared with interpreters' lag time (i.e. the time between delivery of the original message and delivery of the interpreted message). The result shows an inverse relationship between the amount of lag time and the number of interpreter errors. This relationship has serious implications for interpreter educational programs, interpreter assessment programs, and programs intended to make consumers aware of interpreting's limitations.

The interpretation process

Despite limited research on interpretation of signed languages, and of spoken languages, there have been several attempts to understand interpretation through formulation of models for the interpretation process (e.g. Gerver 1976, Moser 1978, Ingram 1974, Ford 1981, Cokely 1985). While there are differences in the sets of factors and characteristics each model addresses, they all view interpretation as a complex cognitive process.

Regardless of which model one accepts, it is clear that the execution and activation of the interpreting process depends upon input that is not controlled by the interpreter; i.e. by the source language (sL) message. It is also clear that the accuracy of any interpretation is directly dependent upon the interpreter's comprehension of the original message—what is not understood cannot be accurately interpreted and what is misunderstood will be misinterpreted.

If the accuracy of an interpretation is related to the interpreter's comprehension, it seems reasonable to ask what are the necessary conditions that will allow accurate comprehension. While it is possible to posit a number of conditions (e.g. familiarity with the subject matter and the speaker), this study will address the question of message processing time, specifically the effects on interpreter errors of lag time (the time between delivery of an original message and the delivery of the interpreted version of that message).

Data base

During the winter of 1983, a national conference was held at the Asilomar Conference Center in Monterey, California. There were approximately 15 presentations during the conference, all of which were interpreted. The data chosen for this study were taken from among the 9 spoken English plenary sessions held during the conference. Each of these sessions was simultaneously interpreted and transliterated for deaf participants. Interpreters were located at stage left (the audience's right), and transliterators were located at stage right. Based on reports from the interpreters, the presence of the transliterators served them as a reminder to interpret and not transliterate.

Permission was obtained from the speakers, interpreters, and transliterators to videotape 10 of the presentations. VHS videotapes of interpreters were made using a professional quality Sony color camera. A simultaneous audio recording of each speaker was made on each videotape, using a directional microphone. For each presentation the camera focused on the interpreter so that the resulting video image was approximately a three-quarters full–body shot. Video cassette work copies were made of each tape and included a digital display of hours, minutes, seconds, and tenths of seconds at the bottom of the picture.

Of the ten interpreters videotaped, four were selected for this study, two with deaf parents (DP) and two with hearing parents (HP). The average age of the four was 33.4 (30 years for DP and 36 years for HP). Both groups have about the same experience as paid interpreters (12.5 years for DP, 12.0 years for HP), and there is relatively little difference in the length of time that members of both groups have held certification from the Registry of Interpreters for the Deaf (8.5 DP, 7.5 HP).

Each of these interpreters worked as a member of a team with another interpreter, relieving each other approximately every twenty minutes. All of the presentations they interpreted can be categorized as spoken English expository monologues. In general each hearing speaker–presenter discussed pertinent research, described personal experiences, and offered practical suggestions. In the data for this study there were no audience comments or questions.

A sampling procedure was used to select the videotaped data to be transcribed for this study: the final minute of each five minute segment of tape available for each interpreter was transcribed. This 20% sampling procedure not only avoided biased selection of a portion of each interpreter's performance but also provided a more realistic indication of each interpreter's overall performance. The procedure yielded a total of 8 minutes of data for each interpreter.

After the work copies were completed and the sample segments identified, two native speakers of English transcribed and verified the audio portion of each tape. A transcription form was used that enabled second–by–second synchronic of the transcription with the digital timing display on the image. An experienced deaf native user of ASL transcribed the interpreters' performances, and working with the author, verified those transcriptions. Speakers' utterances and interpreters' performances were independently transcribed, and only after being verified were they placed on the same transcription form. Conventional orthography was used to transcribe speakers' utterances, and the transcription system described in detail in Baker and Cokely (1980) was used to transcribe interpreters' performance.

Lag time

Because of the cognitive demands of the interpretation process, interpreters cannot immediately begin interpreting when a speaker begins uttering the source language (sL) message. They must wait until they have heard a sufficient portion of the sL message before beginning to produce the target language (tL) rendition. This period of time between the sL utterance and the tL rendition is the interpreter's lag time or "decalage."

Average lag times of 2-3 seconds (Barik 1972) and 10 seconds (Oléron & Nanpon 1965) have been reported, and are largely a function of the structural differences between the sL and the tL. When the structures of the two languages are similar, a shorter lag time may be possible; however, when the structures are signifi-cantly different, a longer lag time is required.

Two of the interpreters in this study (one DP, one HP) had average onset lag times of 2 sec., with ranges of 1-5sec and 1-4sec, respectively. The average onset lag times of the other two interpreters were 4sec for each, with a range of 1-6 seconds. Figure 1 illustrates the maximum, minimum, and average amount of sL information (counted as the number of sL words) available to interpreters.

Given the relationship between comprehension of the sL message and the interpretation's accuracy, it is reasonable to expect that those interpreters who are able to receive more of the sL message before delivering the tL rendition will provide consistently more accurate interpretations. That this is indeed the case can be seen by examining the types and frequency of interpreter miscues.

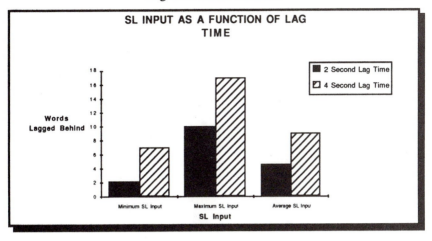

Figure 1. Source language input as a function of lag time.

Interpreter miscues

For an interpretation to be considered accurate or appropriate, the meaning of the sL message must be determined by the interpreter and conveyed in such a way that the meaning is intelligible in the tL. The very nature of the interpretation process makes it possible to determine the extent to which interpreted text tokens adhere to or deviate from the meaning of their sL counterparts. Those instances in which equivalence is not achieved can be considered miscues, i.e. deviations from the original text. More specifically, a miscue is a lack of concordance between the infor-mation in the interpreted tL message and that in the   sL message which it is supposed to convey. While a detailed discussion of interpreter miscues can be found elsewhere (Cokely 1992), the following types of interpreter miscues are germane to this study. (It should be noted that some of the examples that follow contain more than one miscue; however, only the miscue type in question is identified.)

1. *Omissions*
This category refers to instances in which lexically conveyed sL information has been left out of the tL interpretation. While there is no expectation of a one-to-one correspondence

between the sL and tL messages, there is clearly an expectation that the infor-mation conveyed by the sL message will be conveyed in the tL interpretation.

1.1 *Morphological omission*
Content information that is clearly conveyed by bound morphemes in the sL message is omitted:

sL: "...   for the Russian teachers..."

<u>body shift to left   </u>

tL: "...   TEACH   AGENT   RUSSIA......"
              INDEX-rt

Back translation of tL: '... the teacher of Russian...'
Omission: (indication of plural)

1.2 *Lexical omission*

sL: "What do I mean by these policy decisions?"

   <u>nod</u>   <u>brow squint</u>   <u>tl</u>
tL: " POLICY   MEAN #WHAT   "WELL" ..."

Back translation of tL: 'Policy means what? Well...'

Omission: "decisions"

1.3 *Cohesive omission*

sL: "...more or less matching what the matrix told us we wanted. Then we started refining that (the test)..."

tL: "...(2h) THAT GOAL APPROACH , If-SAME-AS-rt

     (eyes head rt.   )
     SCHEDULE _{THAT} HONORIFIC-rt,

     NOW ALMOST If-SAME-AS-rt, (Ihr)   ME,

     START CHANGE++R-E-F-I-N-E CHANGE+++..."

Back translation of tL: "... approaching that goal? It is like the matrix here. Now (?) is almost the same as the matrix. Me? I started changing, refine, changing (something)...

Omission: "...then...that..."

2. *Additions:* This category refers to information that appears in the tL message but not in the original sL message.

2.1 *Nonmanual additions* are nonmanual signals occurring with manual signs that convey information in the tL message different from the intent of the infor-mation in the sL message:

sL: "... an analogy to the simultaneity of listening and speaking in simultaneous (interpretation)..."

```
                                            _____th
tL: "...(2h) 1-CL 'parallel' (1) SAME IDEA RECEIVE-THRU-EAR—..."
      1-----------------                    TALK—
```
Back translation of tL: '...a parallel, similar idea (to) inattentive
       listening and carelessly talking simultaneously...'

```
      _____th
Addition:  "RECEIVE-THRU-EAR"
```

2.2 *Lexical additions* are lexical items in the tL message that add information not in the sL message.

sL: "... If I was studying French history the course would be   taught in French..."

```
                     (eyes up)      _____nod
tL: "IDEA  ME        STUDYwg  ABOUT FRANCE  POSS

                     brow raise/nod   (body shift lft)      _____nod
             CULTURE    "WHOA", ME WILL  (2h)TALKwg FRANCE
                                                   (brow raise)
       _____  nodding
             DURING ME TEACH (1h)THAT INDEX-rt  WELL
```

Back translation of tL: 'Idea I study about France, its culture
       umm I will French while I teach that ? umm...'
Addition: "ME WILL   (2h)TALKwg ... DURING ME TEACH..."

2.3 *Cohesive additions* are items in the tL message that establish reference to or a relation with preceding tL message units not in the sL message.

sL: "...The second task is always designed to distract students' attention from the primary task. An analogy to the simultaneity (of listening and talking)..."

        (body tilt rt)
tL: ...OTHER WORK MUST POINT---OFF-THE-POINT

                                                                           th
PERSON INTERPRET-AGENT If-SHIFT-FOCUS-TO-cntr

                     intense nodding   nodding
MUST INDEX-middle finger   THING,   BECAUSE WANT

(2h)1-CL 'parallel' (1h)SAME IDEA ..."
   1--
Back translation of tL: '...other task must specify--digress,
        person interpreter must carelessly shift attention to [the]
        second thing   because I want [a] parallel, similar idea ...'

Addition: "BECAUSE..."

3. *Substitutions*. This category covers instances in which information contained in the sL message has been replaced in the tL message by information at variance with the intent of the sL message.

3.1 *Expansive substitutions* are tL lexical items that expand or extend the range of meaning of the sL message.

sL: "... If I was studying French history... "

                                                _____nod
tL: ... IDEA ME STUDYwg ABOUT FRANCE POSS CULTURE

Back translation of tL: '[An] idea I study about France, its
        culture...'
Substitution: "...CULTURE..."

3.2 Restrictive substitutions are tL lexical items that restrict or constrict the range of meaning of the sL message.

sL: "... then we started refining that..."

tL: ...ME, START CHANGE++ R-E-F-I-N-E ...
$\qquad$ $\overline{\quad t}$

Back translation of tL: 'Me? I started changing and refining...'

Substitution: "...ME..."
$\qquad$ $\overline{\quad t}$

3.3 Cohesive substitutions are tL lexical items that alter the grammatical cohesive relations intended or estab-lished by the sL message.

sL: "... More importantly I have to decide... "

$\qquad$ (brow raise) $\qquad\qquad\qquad\overline{\text{nodding}}$
tL: ... (2h) ALSO   ME MYSELF-inc MUST DECIDE..."

Back translation of tL: 'Also I myse- -- must decide...'

Substitution: "(2h) ALSO "

3.4 *Unrelated substitutions* are tL lexical items that totally deviate from the sL message and have no immediate sL motivation.

sL: "...but the US [job] market necessitates urgently needs
     interpreters in two languages..."

<pre>
        (body shift rt)   (brow raise   nod))
tL: "TRANSFER-rt WORK FOR C-O-M-M-O-N M-A-R-K-E-T

        (body shift back
        THAT-rt PLACE INDEX-arc PEOPLE MUST* SKILL* TWO
        _____nod
        LANGUAGE+ INTERPRET ..."
</pre>

Back translation of tL: '... transfer to ? work for [the] common
    market that place [of transfer] those people definitely must be
    very skilled interpreting two languages...'

Substitution: "COMMON MARKET..."

4. *Intrusions.* Instances in which the structure of the tL is abandoned and the structure of the sL is adhered to by the interpreter are considered intrusions (of source language grammar into target language).

4.1 *Lexical intrusions* are the "literal" rendering in sL of certain lexical items within an otherwise generally acceptable tL utterance.

sL: "....we [spoken language and sign language interpreters] testify with
     one voice..."

tL: "...US-TWO lf-FIT-IN-rt ONE VOICE..."

Back translation of tL: '...the two of us can merge one voice...'

Intrusion: "...VOICE..."

4.2 Syntactic intrusions are the (almost) total and inappropriate adherence to the syntax of the sL in the production of the tL message, resulting in an in-appropriate and unacceptable utterance.

sL: "... so you have an idea of what I'm trying to get at ..."

                                           <u>nodding</u>
tL: " S-O YOU GET IDEA O-F (1h)"WHAT" MY GOAL "WELL ..."

Back translation of tL: '... so you take possession of an idea of
        what my goal is umm ...'

Intrusion: " ...S-O YOU GET IDEA O-F ..."

5. *Anomalies*. This category refers to instances in which the tL message is meaningless or confused and that cannot be reasonably accounted for or explained by another miscue type.

5.1 *tL utterance anomalies* are meaningless in the tL.

sL: "The matière courses were taken in the other departments..."

                                      (brow raise   )
                                      LIST-OF THINGS
tL: "... SECOND-THING OTHER-inc NEXT

                                          <u>nod</u>
B-index thumb SHIFT-TO INDEX M-A-T-U-R-E

THAT-lf hd INDEX-lf hd   <u>th</u>
5 (base hand)   OTHER P-T-S 5:CL-cntr to lf' ..."

Back translation of tL ' second item in the oth- next list of items the
        first item second item is mature that one there other p-t-s each
        careless p-t-s...'

Anomalies: M-A-T-U-R-E; lack of main verb in tL utterance; lack of
        referent for '5'- - - - .

5.2 Interpretation anomalies are instances in which the tL message either contains a superfluous tL utterance for which there is no sL message motivation, or omits significant portions of the sL message.

sL: "... looking at curriculum designed in such a way means that I'm going to address also six content considerations ..."

<u>nodding</u>
tL: "... THAT MY FEEL ABOUT LIST-OF "WAIT A MINUTE"

<u>   nod   nodding   cond</u>
IF WE FOLLOW THAT IDEA+ IDEA-EXPAND FOR LIST-OF

<u>   (head down</u>
WE MUST-inc "WELL" MUST FOCUS-ONcntr/rt SIX

)
(2H) IDEA-alt THINK ABOUT WHAT WILL INCLUDE IN*

        (body shift right
THAT LIST-OF ME WANT ME EXPLAIN ABOUT THAT SIX

)
LIST-OF..."

Back translation of tL: '... that is my feeling about the list of items—wait now—if we follow those ideas and the expanded idea for the list of items there we mus— well focus on <u> ? </u> six ideas think about what will be included in that list of items that I want to explain that six list of items ...'

Anomalies: initial and final portions of the tL message.

Miscues & lag time

Having detailed the types of miscues, we can now examine the relationship between miscues by type and lag time. Figure 2 presents the overall distri-bution of major miscue

categories. Throughout this discussion, miscue occurrences
are presented as an average of each pair. In no instance did
any of the interpreters deviate from the reported average by
more than 5 miscues. As Figure 2 shows, the interpreters
with a 2-second lag time had more than twice the total
number of miscues made by the interpreters with a 4-second
lag; and these had almost twice as many miscues as those
with a 6-second lag. In addition, the number of miscues in
each category was greater for the pair with the shorter lag
time.

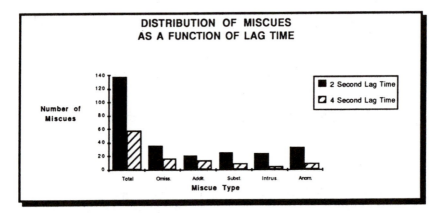

Figure 2. Distribution of miscues as a
function of lag time.

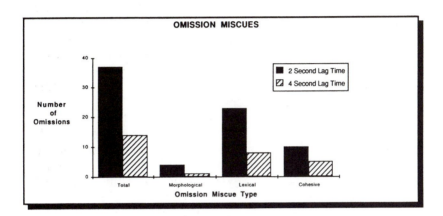

Figure 3.   Distribution of omissions as a
function of lag time.

Lag time & omissions. Figure 3 presents the data on omissions. Lexical omissions are the most frequent for both pairs. Again it is worth noting that there are more than twice as many total miscues for those interpreters with the shorter lag time and that this ration holds across all subcategories; however, while frequency information is revealing, it does not necessarily mirror the significance of these subcategories.

One might argue that lexical omissions, although infrequent, are less severe than cohesive or morpho-logical omissions. Certainly the possibility that the consumers might apply cloze skills (i.e. complete partial messages) is greater for lexical than other kinds of omissions. Additionally, depending on the nature of the omitted information, the overall meaning of the tL interpretation may be only slightly different from that of the sL message. This is in no way meant to diminish the importance of lexical omissions, however. It is simply to underscore the possibility that consumers will find morphological and cohesive omissions more difficult to repair than lexical omissions. Indeed, while certain instances of lexical omission may result in meaningless or questionable tL utterances (which presumably would be identified by consumers and dealt with accordingly), morphological and cohesive omis-sions generally yield utterances that are meaningful and cannot be readily repaired by consumers.

A naive or uninformed view of simultaneous inter-pretation might hold that the shorter the lag time between sL message and tL interpretation, the less likelihood that the interpreter will omit information. However, the data presented here run counter to that notion. It would seem that increased lag time enhances overall comprehension of the sL message and allows the interpreter to determine the informational and functional value of morpho-logical and cohesive as well as lexical units. Conversely, a compressed lag time places the interpreter in a quasi-shadowing task, in which differences in speech articulation and sign pro-duction rates may result in increased omissions, as the interpreter strives to "keep up" with the speaker.

Lag time & additions. Figure 4 presents the data on addition miscues. Again, note that there is twice the number of miscues for the pair of interpreters with a 2-second lag time than for those with a 4-second lag time.

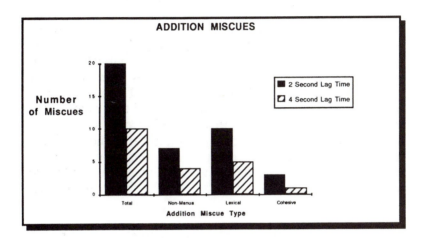

Figure 4. Addition miscues as a function of lag time.

As with omissions, it is useful to examine additions from the perspective of the consumer's ability to recover the intended sL meaning from a tL message to which information has been added. Clearly if a lexical addition results in a meaningless tL message, the consumer is alerted that something has gone awry. However, in order to recover the meaning intended in the sL message, the consumer would have to identify the addition and delete it from the tL message. It is unlikely that consumers would be able to do this consistently or that this would be their first response. Indeed, consumers may respond by assuming that an omission has occurred, in which case they might rely on their cloze skills and perhaps compound the effect of the miscue.

The subcategory of nonmanual additions is particularly interesting. By far the two most frequent added nonmanual behaviors are the 'th' and 'mm' In fact, these two account for 73% of the nonmanual additions. A possible explanation is that there may be certain manual signs and nonmanual behaviors that were erroneously learned (or acquired) by the interpreters and perceived by them as single entities. Thus the production automatically results in the non-manual behavior the interpreter assumes is "required." A less satisfying explanation is that these behaviors are used by interpreters in order to "look as if" they are using the tL. If this were indeed the motivation for the nonmanual additions, one would expect them to be more frequent than they are. The relatively limited occurrence of nonmanual additions would seem to suggest that some other factor motivates them (i.e. the failure to view these behaviors as distinct from the manual signs they accompany).

Lag time & substitutions. Figure 5 presents the occurrence of substitution miscues. Here it is worth noting that the total number of substitution miscues for those interpreters with a 2-second lag time is more than four times that for those with a 4-second lag time. As with addition miscues, substitution miscues generally offer the consumer very little possibility (a) of recognizing that the tL interpretation differs from the sL message, and (b) of recovering or retrieving the intended sL meaning. The primary reason for this is that substitutions do not automatically result in ungrammatical tL utterances nor, save in a few cases of unrelated substitutions, a tL utterance that is semantically marked. Thus, lacking syntactic or semantic information to the contrary, the consumer can only accept the tL utterance "at face value."

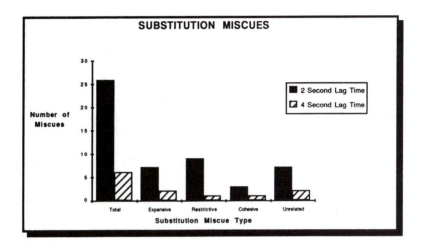

Figure 5. Substitution miscues as a function of lag time.

Clearly not all instances of substitutions are equally serious for the consumer. Expansive and restrictive substitutions, while not rendering the exact equivalent of the sL message, are nevertheless not totally unrelated to the sL meaning. Of the two, restrictive substitutions would seem to be less troublesome, as the TL substitution, although it does not convey as much information as intended in the sL message, does not add information to, or overextend, the sL intent. In terms of intended meaning, then, restrictive substitution results in parts being conveyed for wholes, while expansive substitutions result in wholes being conveyed for parts. Thus a consumer acting on the basis of a tL message containing an expansive substitution might frequently be in error. On the other hand, a consumer acting on the basis of a tL message containing a restrictive substitution would rarely be in error. (The consumer would not, however, be as "correct" as those receiving the intact sL message.)

Intrusions & lag time. Figure 6 provides data on intrusion miscues. That the occurrence of intrusion miscues is five times greater for the pair with the shorter lag time should not be surprising. Lexical intrusions are likely to occur because the interpreter lacks sufficient comprehension of the sL message with which to determine appropriate tL lexical selection; and syntactic intrusions occur because the interpreter is temporally constrained to the syntactic structures of the sL. A longer lag time increases the possibility that the interpreter will accurately comprehend a greater portion of the sL message before determining lexical selection, and it at least makes more possible the production of syntactically appropriate tL utterances—or at a minimum, more tL–like utterances.

Syntactic intrusions present several problems to consumers, all of which decrease the likelihood that the sL–based tL utterance will be accurately understood. The obvious difficulty is that accurate comprehension of such utterances is directly related to competence in the sL. The very presence of an interpreter, however, is an indication that at least some of the consumers either lack competence in the sL or prefer not to test their competence by dealing more directly with the sL (as they would do if they watched the transliterator instead of the interpreter). A second problem arises because syntactic intrusions occur rather randomly and intermittently. The result may be a type of cognitive and linguistic dissonance for the consumer that can only be resolved if the consumer is capable of and engages in what can be called retrospective code-switching. However, consumers thus engaged are not able to attend fully to subsequent portions of the tL interpretation. A third problem has to do with the cumulative effects of such intrusions (and indeed of miscues in general if perceived by consumers) on the level of confidence consumers have in the interpreter. If miscues of this type erode consumer confidence, then the interpreter's performance will continue to be questioned even when no such miscues are evident.

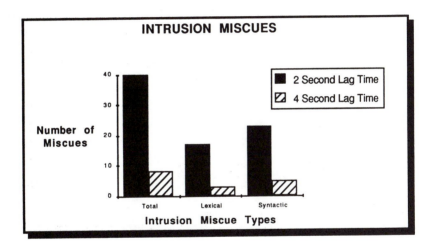

Figure   6. Intrusion miscues as a function of lag   time.

Anomalies & lag time. Figure 7 presents the distribution of anomaly miscues. Again there are four times as many anomaly miscues for the pair of interpreters with the shorter time lag. It is true that tL utterance anomalies might be accounted for by applying several of the preceding miscue categories. While theoretically intriguing, it is more efficient and efficacious to avoid such post facto rationalizations ("first add this, then delete that, then substitute this ..."). Not only is such a procedure cumbersome, but there very likely would be several equally plausible routes to the same results. Thus it seems appropriate to treat these miscues as anomalies.

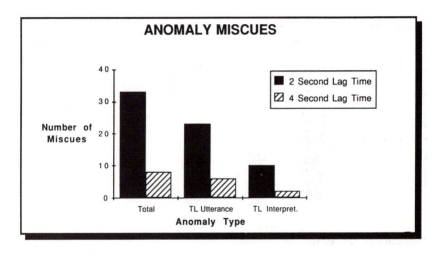

Figure 7. Anomaly miscues as a function of lag time.

As might be expected, anomalies inherently present several serious problems for consumers. Those who can identify tL utterance anomalies will likely be unable to determine the exact cause of the meaningless tL utterance and in the process of trying to render such utterances meaningful, may distort even further their understanding of the original message. Consumers presented with a tL interpretation anomaly will likely be totally unaware of the miscue. Consequently, consumers can only take such utterances as expressing the intent of the original sL message. In both cases the consumer is presented with a formidable challenge in trying to recover the original sL message: in the case of tL utterance anomalies the consumer mus extract meaning from a syntactically meaningless utterance; in the case of tL interpretation anomalies the consumer must already know the sL message in order to determine what was added or omitted.

Lexical & syntactic level miscues

In order to examine the full impact and extent of miscues, it will be helpful to re-analyze the miscue types presented above as occurring at either the lexical or the syntactic level. Such an analysis will not only provide a more accurate understanding of the extent of miscues but will also more clearly illustrate the relationship between lag time and miscue occurrence.

Figure 8 shows the average total number of tL sentences produced by each pair of interpreters in the eight minute sampling period. This table also shows the number of those sentences that are acceptable (i.e. are syntactically correct in the tL), and the number containing syntactic–level miscues. The data reveal that of the total number of tL sentences produced by those interpreters with a 2-second time lag, 40% contain a syntactic level miscue. It is also worth noting that those interpreters with a longer lag time not only produced a greater total number of tL sentences but also a greater number that were acceptable. An obvious explanation is that those with longer lag time simply had more time in which to analyze incoming sL message units and to formulate acceptable tL expressions for those message units.

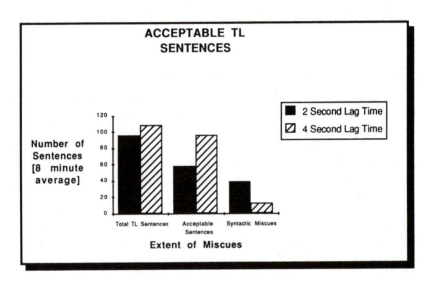

Figure 8. Number of acceptable sentences by lag time.

As discussed above, miscues at the syntactic level are particularly serious for consumers: recovery is dependent either upon competence in the source language or upon prior knowledge of the sL message. Even if one were to argue that consumers possess sufficient competence in the sL to compensate for such miscues, the information in Figure 9 shows that such competence would allow consumers to recover from less than half of all syntactic level miscues. The majority of syntactic miscues for both pairs of interpreters are anomalies—in tL utterance and in tL interpretation.

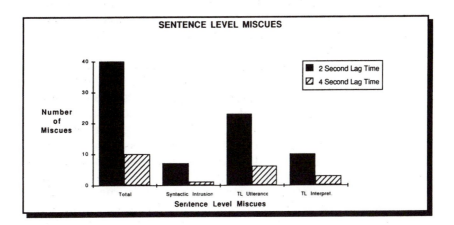

Figure   9.   Sentence–level   miscues   by   lag
time.

It is worth noting that those interpreters with a 2-second lag time exhibit four times as many syntactic level miscues as those with a 4-second lag time. In the case of syntactic intrusions, this dramatic difference may be explained by the fact that with a reduced lag time the interpreter is engaged in performing a quasi–shadowing task, necessarily constrained to the syntactic structures of the Source Language.

Syntactic level miscues are not the only obstacle to consumer recovery of intended sL meaning, although they are probably the most severe obstacle with which consumers must contend. Lexical level miscues are also problems for consumers. Although one could argue that consumers might recover the intended meaning of a single lexical miscue in an otherwise appropriate tL utterance, this assumes that the consumers are aware that a miscue has occurred and are aware of the type of miscue. However, since consumers are almost inherently unaware of the occurrence and type of miscue, it is unlikely that the intended sL meanings can be consistently and accurately recovered. This especially true when one considers the frequency with which lexical level miscues occur.

It is true that consumers can more easily recover from certain types of lexical level miscues than from others. For example, certain lexical omissions might be recoverable from context. But certain types of lexical level miscues are quite resistant to recovery of intended sL meaning; e.g. lexical additions or unrelated substitutions are less recoverable because there is generally no indication that they have occurred; consumers are less likely to notice them because the resulting tL utterance may be inherently meaningful. Recognition of such "non–recoverable" miscues requires prior knowledge of the sL message, which is generally unavailable to consumers. Figure 10 presents the frequency and types of such "non–recoverable" lexical miscues.

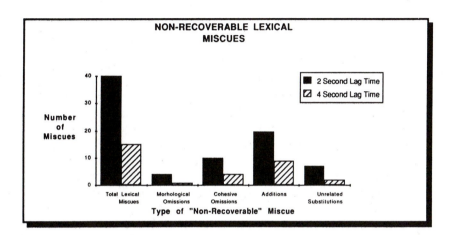

Figure   10. Non–recoverable   lexical miscues.

The data in Figure 10 make it clear that recovery of intended sL meaning from "serious" lexical miscues is a formidable task for consumers. (Of course the cumulative effects of losing intended sL meanings and of the expense of cognitive efforts in the recovery process are not known; further research in this area is needed.) Again it is worth noting that those interpreters with a shorter lag time exhibit almost three times as many non-recoverable lexical miscues as do those with a longer lag time.

When non–recoverable lexical miscues and syntactic level miscues are considered together, the extent of "serious" miscues becomes clear. With 2-second lag time, 80 "serious" miscues amount to one "serious" miscue every 1. 2 tL sentences, or one "serious" miscue every 0. 73 of an acceptable tL sentence. With 4-second lag time, 25 "serious" miscues amount to one "serious" miscue every 4.3 tL sentences, or one "serious" miscue for every 3.8 acceptable tL sentences.

Of course these calculations assume that "serious" lexical and syntactic level miscues are equally distributed across all sentences, but they are not. Nevertheless, these calculations do provide an indication of the challenge confronting consumers attempting to recover from miscue laden tL sentences and to extract the intended sL meaning from the interpreted utterances. When both "serious" (i.e. non–recoverable) and "non–serious" (recoverable) miscues are thus considered, the full extent of the challenge consumers face becomes clear: with 2-second lag time 137 total miscues amount to one miscue every 0. 7 of a tL sentence, or one miscue every 0.4 of an acceptable tL sentence (i.e. more than two miscues per sentence). With 4-second lag time, 58 total miscues amount to one miscue every 1.9 tL sentences, or one miscue every 1.7 acceptable tL sentences.

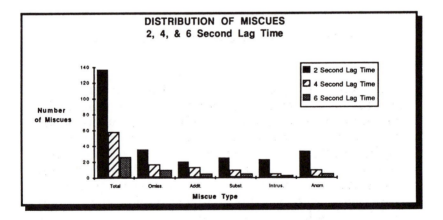

Figure   11. Distribution of miscues by 2, 4,
and 6-sec. lag time.

As the data in Figure 11 indicate, the single interpreter
with a 6-second lag time had less than half as many total
miscues as the interpreters with a 4-second lag time. The
number of miscues in each category decreases as the lag time
of the interpreters increases. There is not a single category or
subcategory in which this pattern is broken or reversed. The
constancy of this pattern seems to indicate that the greater the
lag time, the more the interpreter is able to comprehend the
original sL message because of having more of the message
with which to work.

This is not to say, however, that there is no upper limit to lag
time; interpreters, after all, are only human. It is likely that
for some individuals there is a lag time threshold beyond
which the number of omissions would significantly increase
because the threshold is at the upper limits of the individual's
short–term working memory.

Summary

This study has examined the relationship between lag time
and miscues in interpreted material. The data here were all
drawn from simultaneous interpretation of presentations at a
professional conference—arguably the most demanding and
difficult setting in which interpretation occurs. (It is quite
likely that in other interpreting situations the frequency of the
miscues would be different, although the same relationship
between lag time and miscues would be found.) These data
provide evidence of a definite relationship between the lag
time and miscue occurrence: *as the degree of temporal
synchrony between the sL message and tL interpretation
increases, so does the frequency of miscues.* The primary
reason for this is the quantity of the sL message available to
the interpreter. The greater the lag time, the more information
available; the more information available, the greater the level
of comprehension. Clearly there is a temporal threshold
below which sufficient information cannot be available to the
interpreter.

This study has certain implications for interpreters and
consumers. For interpreters it may mean that in certain
situations there is need for an external monitor of

performance; the more serious the consequences of interpreter miscues are to the consumer (e.g. a legal setting), the more essential is such external monitoring. This external monitoring can only be provided by another interpreter, because competence in both sL and tL is necessary to identify miscues. For consumers an obvious implication is that certain instances of misunderstanding may be due not to their own cognitive limitations but rather to the skewed tL input that they receive. Another implication for consumers is an understanding that accurate interpretation requires sufficient sL information. Consumers who demand that interpreters "keep up with the speaker" are requiring them to do the very thing that will produce inaccurate interpretation.

Clearly there are a number of important questions unanswered by this study (e.g. the cumulative effects of miscues on consumers' comprehension, the strategies used by interpreters with longer lag time to "chunk" sL information). It is hoped that this study provides a useful point of departure for addressing these and other aspects of interpretation.

REFERENCES

Baker, C. & D. Cokely
  1980 *American Sign Language: A Teacher's Resource Text on Grammar & Culture.* Silver Spring MD: T.J. Publishers.
Barik, H.
  1972 *Simultaneous Interpretation: Temporal & Quantitative Data.* UNC, Thurstone Psychometric Laboratory, Working Paper 103,
Cokely, D.
  1985 Towards a sociolinguistic model of the interpreting process: Focus on ASL &

English. Unpublished dissertation,
Georgetown University.
[*Interpretation: A Sociolinguistic Model*
Linstok Press, 1992]

Ford, R.
1981 The interpreter as a communication
specialist. In *Proceedings of the 3rd
International Symposium on Interpretation
of Sign Languages.* London: Royal
National Institute for the Deaf.

Gerver, D.
1976 Empirical studies of simultaneous
interpretation: A review & a model. In
Translation: Applications & Research,
Gerver & Sinaiko eds. New York: Gardner
Press. 165-207.

Ingram, R.
1974 A communication model of the interpreting
process, *Journal of Rehabilitation of the
Deaf* (January), 3-9.

Moser, B.
1978 Simultaneous interpretation: A hypothetical
model & its practical application. *In
Language Interpretation & Communication,*
Gerver & Sinaiko eds. New York: Plenum
Press. 353-368.

Oléron, P. & H. Nanpon
1964 Récherches sur la traduction simultanée.
*Journal de Psychologie Normale et
Pathologique* 62, 73-94.

V. Determining Register

in Sign-to-English Interpreting

Risa Shaw

Abstract

The notion of style or register for general communication studies has not yet received the direct and sustained focus that it deserves. There are numerous linguistic and sociolinguistic indicators of a particular communicative register. This fact alone has significant implications for Sign Language interpreters. This study represents an initial effort to explore the manner in which Sign Language interpreters address the complex question of register in the source texts with which they work. Because the accuracy of an interpreted message is directly dependent upon the interpreter's comprehension of the source text, this initial study also yields specific implications for interpreter preparation programs.

Register in discourse

Register is a discourse variable of immense importance in making communication possible, but because it involves knowledge that several different disciplines claim as their own it has not been studied as much as its importance warrants. Linguists can claim that such linguistic variables as syntax, lexicon, phonology help set and maintain register. Paralinguistic features are also directly involved; e.g. intonation, pausing, and rate of speaking. But social variables—context, setting, the participants in the discourse—operate both with and apart from linguistic ones. Psychology enters as well, particularly in the process of deciding among alternate behaviors and judging their effects.

Sociolinguistics helps in uniting these disparate analyses of register, for its field is that of discourse functions and the ways these interact with each other and with social factors.

Although register has received little direct and sustained attention, the following remarks may help to make clear what is meant by register. Wardhaugh refers to several distinguishing features:

People do have a wide range of choices available to them when they speak: they can be technical or non-technical, formal or informal, conscious of their role or unconscious of it, familiar with the listener or distant; and so on. The consequences will show in the language they use; the amount of technical terminology employed; the kinds of omissions made and tolerated; the types and complexity of grammatical constructions; the standards of grammatical "accuracy" observed. (1976).

Bolinger adds to this list the importance of tone of voice, or intonation (1975). McEdwards describes register as "the product of [one's] conscious and unconscious selection of the topic, the organization, the diction, the vocabulary, the syntax, and the imagery allowed [one] by [one's] premises to communicate [one's] emotions and ideas" (1968).

In his 1961 book *The Five Clocks,* Martin Joos, who refers to register as style, makes a very useful division into five levels. (Presumably because "style" has come to have so many meanings, the word *register* is currently preferred for the matter in hand.) A brief listing of the definitions by Joos follows:

Frozen style is characteristic of poetry and liturgy; not a word can be changed; ambiguity is its special form of politeness;

Formal style is marked by personal detachment, cohesion of form and organization, absence of participation, explicit pronunciation, grammar that tolerates no ellipsis, careful semantics, and a clear intention to inform;

Consultative style also intends to be informative but supplies background information, includes the addressee(s) in participation, has complete grammar and clear pronunciation;

Casual style is marked by ellipsis and slang (participants are on first–name terms and can supply what is left out); background information is likewise absent; there is little reliance on listener participation but treatment of the addressee as an "insider;"

Intimate style is a personal code shared only by those using it and is full of jargon and omissions that would puzzle others.

Most of the time sign language interpreters work in the middle three levels, of register, although Joos's frozen style might be appropriate in interpreting certain rituals. (The kind of relationship calling for communication in intimate style excludes any third party, even an interpreter, by definition.)

Register is a complicated phenomenon. Its numerous indicators are neither isolated nor static. It is a combination of linguistic, sociological, and psycho-logical factors, some or all of which may determine the register a communicating person uses at any time. This is not to imply that register is impossible to investigate but only to warn that there is rarely an absolute.

The investigation reported here is an attempt to identify indicators of register in selected portions of two lectures presented in ASL, and in the inter-pretations of each made by two interpreters. The results are used to suggest desiderata for training interpreters.

The data

Ideally one would be able to determine register immediately and directly from live discourse, but to do so might well require a large part of a lifetime; therefore, in this preliminary attempt to describe register in interpreted material I have used videotaped material, but material so structured that many of the important sociolinguistic variables can be known. The data tapes are professionally produced by Sign Media, Incorporated of Burtonsville, MD (*Interpreter Models Series: ASL–English: Lectures*). The series includes two tapes so far, the first presenting interpretation from English to ASL, and the second, used in this study, interpretation from ASL to English.

The producers of the tapes first recorded two half-hour lecture presentations by two Deaf speakers along with two simultaneous interpretations of each. For the final product, they then selected from each a segment of about eight minutes, in which one can watch: (a) the Deaf lecturer's presentation only, (b) that presentation with one spoken interpretation on the sound track, or (c) the same presentation with the other interpreter's voice audible.

The Deaf signer–presenters were chosen because they were experienced in Sign presentation to an audience, in working with interpreters, and had grown up using ASL. Both are in their 30s, have masters' degrees in education, teach deaf students, have Deaf parents, and are bilingual in ASL and written English. The producers asked them to give 20–30 minute talks on a topic they were comfortable with. They were asked not to read from a paper and to be as extemporaneous as possible. Speaker–signer 1, female, gave a linguistic and cultural discussion of teaching English through ASL. Speaker–signer 2, male, gave a narrative account of his experiences as a househusband.

Nine hearing and five deaf persons were invited by the producers to be the speakers' audience. The nine hearers were not acquainted with signing and had to depend on the interpreter; the five deaf participants were fluent in ASL. Filming took place in a specially prepared room. Speaker and podium were on a platform 18 inches above floor level. A collapsible partition split the room in such a way that the speaker could see the people on both sides, but they could not see each other. Thus two interpreters for the speaker could interpret simultaneously for the two halves of the audience, each of which was made up of hearing and deaf persons. The interpreters and the deaf part of the audience had a clear view of the speaker; the non-signing hearing audience was positioned near enough the interpreter to hear clearly.

The interpreters wore headphones to prevent hearing each other's voices and spoke into a separate microphone directly linked to the audio recording equipment. They were selected for their national reputations, the producers' knowledge of their capabilities, experience in conference interpreting, and their commitment to the field. Both were in their 30s at the time of filming; both are bilingual native users of ASL and English with deaf parents; and both have at least eighteen years of professional interpreting experience and ten years experience in training interpreters. Both are considered to be at the top of their profession nationally by the interpreting and Deaf communities.

Interpreter A was born and raised on the East coast, holds a master's degree in counseling, and is currently completing a Ph.D. dissertation in linguistics. *Interpreter B* was born and raised in the Southwest and on the West coast, holds a master's degree in education, and has done interdisciplinary work on the Ph.D. level.

Determining ASL registers

Verification of the source message register was the first step taken, in order to compare the interpretation register with the original, to determine influence of the source register on the interpretation register, and to examine the interpreters' ability to manipulate register indicators. A native ASL user, who is a qualified and recognized expert in ASL linguistics examined the videotapes of the speaker–signers and judged that *Speaker 1* stayed consistently in an upper consultative register. The grounds for this determination are: the topic (linguistics), genre (lecture), goal (to persuade), presentation of background information (interpreter did not assume listener knowledge), crisp "pronuciation" (careful sign and manual letter production), reliance on audience comprehension signals (eye contact seeking indications a chunk of information was understood), controlled but present "intonation" (subdued affective signals of face and body, and force of signs), consistent use of space (distinct and deliberate placement of topics and nouns), non-rapid delivery (relative low speed of signing), and a cohesive and organized presentation (clear and connected points).

The same judge determined that *Speaker 2*, who was giving a personal account of his experiences as a househusband, was generally in an upper casual register, although he often shifted into consultative register. The grounds for this determination are: the topic (staying at home with his son), genre (personal narrative), goal (to entertain), absence of background information (assuming listener knowledge), little reliance on audience participation (brief eye contact with individual members of the audience), increased ASL "intonation" (distinct and shifting affective signals of face and body and force of signs and body movement), rapid delivery (fast signing and fingerspelling throughout, except for slowing for emphasis), less organized presentation (numerous asides), and strong use of dialogue (impersonating the characters in the narrative).

Analysis

For analysis I chose a segment two minutes and 27 seconds long from Speaker 1's presentation, and another two minutes and 17 seconds long from Speaker 2's. These provided a cohesive piece of discourse, several subtopics within the segment, sufficient data buy a manageable size for analysis, and little culture–bound information that would have forced difficult decisions on the interpreters. The 147 and 137 seconds of tape provided an overwhelming amount of data to be considered as pertinent to register. I consequently adjusted the depth of the analysis to the scope of the project.

I used conventional orthography in transcribing the data. Phonetic transcription would have provided much unneeded information but did note certain phonetic features; e.g. assimilation (gonna, wanna) and elongation of syllables (s-speak). I coded for the following keys to register: intonation, pausing, lexical items, increase in speech rate, and sentence boundaries. I also took note of laughter, individual word stress, and run–together words. All transcription work was performed by native English users, and intonation was evaluated by a recognized expert in phonology. (The Appendix gives the complete transcripts of all four interpretation segments.) Pausing data was coded by ear and stopwatch to 0.1 sec. accuracy, and it was deemed that 0.4 seconds was a significant delineation point. Stress on individual words, laughter, run–together words, change in speech rate, and sentence boundaries were identified by native–speaker intuition.

Five categories seemed worthy of special attention after I became familiar with the data: *speaking rate, pausing, syntax, intonation*, and *lexical choice*. Each was analyzed separately and as related to each other, also for each interpreter across speakers. When differences between interpreters appeared, these were compared and contrasted. The categories are presented and discussed below.

Interpreter speaking rate was calculated by counting the number of words in the selection and dividing by the time. The rate of the speaker-signers' original performance was not calculated, although it may be of interest in a related study; and as shown by interpreter rate, the speaker-signers' rates were different:

Table 1. Rate by speaker & interpreter in words/minute.

	Speaker 1	Speaker 2
Interpreter A	167.92wpm	210.43wpm
Interpreter B	173.47wpm	225.53wpm

It appears that both interpreters increased their rate of speaking because of Speaker 2's more rapid rate of signing (25.32% and 30.01% respectively). The increase in speaking rate is fully in accord with the difference in register of the two presentations.

Pauses are not considered in the calculations of speaking rate but were measured and counted and total pause time calculated for each interpreter:

The total number of pauses across speakers is similar, with nearly 90% of all pauses being 1.6 seconds or shorter in length. Interpreter A, however, used many more long pauses than did Interpreter B, and all but one of her long pauses were made during her interpretation of Speaker 1's presentation. I take this as a strong indication in A's interpretation of the register difference between speakers, but see below. The percentage of actual speaking time (seconds of speaking, *ss*) and pause time (seconds of pausing, *sp*) is shown in Table 3:

Table 2. Interpreters' pauses by speaker.

Pauses < 1sec	Spkr 1	Spkr 2	Totals	Both
Interpreter A	32	43	75	161
Interpreter. B	42	44	86	89.94%
Pauses >1.6 sec				
Interpreter A	15	1	16	18
Interpreter. B	2	0	2	10.06%
Total pauses				
Interpreter A	47	44	91	179
Interpreter. B	44	44	88	100%

Table 3. Percentage of speaking and pausing time.

	Speaker 1		Speaker 2	
	Interp. A	Interp .B	Interp. A	Interp .B
ss	60.9	74.01	78.04	82.13 %
ps	39.10	25.99	21.96	17.87 %

Both interpreters are speaking a smaller part of the total time for Speaker 1, another indication that 1 uses a more formal register than Speaker 2, allowing more time for audience comprehension, signing slower, and using crisper pronunciation. Again Interpreter A's pause rate appears different across speakers; her overall pause time for Speaker 1 is considerably greater than that in the rest of the 'ps' line.
Syntax: Syntactic difference was assessed by noting sentences as simple and non-simple (i.e. compound, complex, and compound-complex) In Interpreter A's rendering there were 19 sentences for Speaker 1 and 35 for Speaker 2. Interpreter used 26 sentences for S. 1 and 44 for

S. 2. Table 4 shows that judged by the proportion of simple and non-simple syntactic structures used by both interpreters, Speaker 2 is being interpreted in a more casual register than is Speaker 1. It also appears that less complex syntax, with greater speaking rate and smaller pause time, leads to greater speed.

Table 4 . Percentages of simple and non-simple S's.

	Speaker 1		Speaker 2		
	Interp. A	Interp .B	Interp. A	Interp. B	
simp	32	42	46	61	(54)
non-s	68	58	54	38	(46)

I also examined as part of the syntactic analysis false starts and non-agreement between subject and verb Coherent organization and grammatical accuracy as indicators of more formal register show again the difference of register in the speakers. These indicators, however, may be affected by interpreter performance; Interpreter A makes more false starts in interpreting for Speaker 2, but the reverse is true of Interpreter B.

Table 5. False starts & non-agreement across spkrs.

	False starts		Non-agreement	
	Sprk 1	Spkr 2	Spkr 1	Spkr 2
Interpreter A	2	10	2	3
Interpreter B	16	9	0	4

Intonation. Roach (1983) lists four functions of intonation: *attitudinal,* conveying emotions and attitudes; *accentual,* denoting prominence and stress; *grammatical,* indicating features of syntax and grammar; *discourse,* signaling expectation of flow and turn-taking. He describes the semantics of intonation patterns thus: A fall is "associated with completeness and definiteness," a rise, with "incompleteness and uncertainty or questioning," a fall-rise, with "feelings of hesitation, contrast, reservation, or doubt," a rise-fall, with "strong feelings of approval, disapproval, or surprise," and a wider pitch range "tends to be used in excited or enthusiastic speaking."

Bolinger (1975) corroborates by explaining this within the context of the physiology of speech and the nervous system. He states that the "universal lowering of pitch towards the ends of unexcited discourse results automatically from running out of lung power," and that an "equally universal raising of pitch for questions and other keyed-up utterances is probably the result of higher nervous tension in the body as a whole, which has the effect of tensing the vocal cords."

The number of occurrences and their locations of rising and falling intonation within a syllable or larger unit were charted for the interpreters' performances, and are shown in Table 6.

I expected to find more intonation shifts in both interpretations of Speaker 2 because of his highly affect-laden personal narratives, but Table 6 indicates otherwise. The interpreters agree closely on Speaker 2, but for Speaker 1, Interpreter B has 27.2% more intonation shifts than she does for Speaker 2. This would not be expected from the literature on intonation and may indicate a problem in control of intonation for more formal registers, or it may come from an idiosyncrasy of the interpreter. Interpreter A shows more intonation shifts than Interpreter B for Speaker 2, and she distinguishes between registers across speakers by her use of intonation patterns. This seems to indicate that more formal registers require greater control of intonation; while a greater range is allowed and accepted within less formal registers.

Lexical items: Categories of lexical items examined were contractions (e.g. *I'd*), phonetic assimilations (*gonna*) , repairs and repetitions, the word and, and more formal and less formal words and phrases.

Table 6. Interpreter pitch changes across speakers.

	Speaker 1		Speaker 2	
	Interpreter A	Interpreter B	Interpreter A	Interpreter B
Total	92	145 100%	115	114 100%
Falls	71 77%	97 67%	79 69%	78 69%
Rises	21 23%	48 33%	36 31%	36 31%

We can see that both of the interpretations of Speaker 2 are more formal in diction than those of Speaker 1, but the lexical evidence is not consistent across interpreters and so is not a conclusive indicator of difference in organization and cohesion of the discourse interpreted; e.g. Interpreter A shows a 120% increase in repairs and repetitions from Speaker 1 to Speaker 2, which does indicate a register difference in her interpretations. Indeed Interpreter A's register difference between speakers throughout shows a greater register difference than does Interpreter B's.

Table 7. Interpreters' lexical patterns.

	Total	Int. A	Int. B	Total	Int. A	Int. B
contract'ns	19	12	7	32	15	17
assimil'ns	1	1	1	24	17	7
repetitions	15	5	10	19	11	8
and	28	13	15	54	26	28
- formal	50	17	33	101	52	49
+ formal	80	49	31	31	17	14

Summary

The analysis clearly shows that both interpreters used different registers for the two signed presentations. It also indicates a greater difference in register across speakers in the interpretation of Interpreter A. Both interpretations show the following properties indicative of their register. For Speaker 1 there was more pause time, crisper pronunciation, and more complex syntax in the work of both interpreters. For Speaker 2 in both interpretations there was faster speaking rate, use of more contractions, assimilations, more use of *and,* more informal words and phrases, and simpler syntactic structures.

A's interpretation differed more from speaker to speaker than B's; specifically containing greater shifts in speaking rate, more pause time, intonation change, and syntax, difference, as well as fewer false starts—11 repetitions and repairs interpreting Speaker 1 as against 5 interpreting Speaker 2.

Interpreter B made less distinct adjustments and showed greater inconsistency in registers across speakers, with more false starts and more intonation shifts for Speaker 1 than for Speaker 2 but less adjustment in syntactic structure and pause time.

Both interpretations included aspects of con-sultative and casual register as did both presen-tations by the original speakers, but there were differences in register indicators in the inter-pretations, implying that registers exist within ranges and have definable properties but lack discrete boundaries. Any given utterance will present itself as more or less in "X register," depending on its aspects and their inter-action. Thus, the attempt to isolate and define register indicators so that they can be monitored and regulated in the interpreting process appears quite feasible, and consistency is essential to register determination.

A multitude of factors are involved in interpre-tation; and perhaps some such description as this of register indicators (and knowledge that consistency in their use is essential) may reduce some of the stress that many problems of interpretation impose on interpreters and their audiences.

Implications for interpreter training

Register as text variety is 'embedded' in situation. It reflects individual experience...control of a range of different registers results from experiencing different kinds of situations demanding different kinds of behaviour. (Gregory & Carroll 1978)

Ability to act effectively as interpreter in any situation is directly related to the interpreter's experience and knowledge. As Gregory and Carroll put it, the ability to manage register is no exception, and interpreters to comprehend and express registers appropriately need to have experienced a range of them. Training procedures should sharpen the students' ability to recognize individuals' use of register indicators, to expand their own range and regulating behaviors, and to monitor their own language performance in different kinds of communicative situations as well as during actual interpretation. Special attention needs to be given those indicators foreign to or not in the usual behavior of each student, and to the importance of the way indicators can act on one another as well as on the overall message.

Ideally students of interpreting would acquire skill in register control through actual experiences in their lives, but most do not enter training programs with such background, nor can they be "given" the experience. Therefore, curriculum must be developed to address these needs specifically. The students need to be exposed to the linguistic behaviors and the opportunity to try them out in and out of the classroom.

Register is as well the realization of the semantic possibilities of language. It defines what can be meant in the situation. Register is, then, culturally determined, since it is the culture of a society which determines the patterns of environments in which language can occur. (Gregory & Carroll 1978)

This point must never be forgotten, especially not by those who train interpreters. Register analysis must be done separately in each language—English and ASL—so as not to cause interference or confusion about how the culture of the users of each language determines what register is appropriate for what occasions. Register, as with all linguistic and sociological aspects of communi-cation, must always be considered in context while realizing its dynamic nature. Interpretation itself is dynamic.

REFERENCES

Bolinger, D.
  1975 *Aspects of Language.* (2nd ed) NY: Harcourt.

Gregory, M. & S. Carroll
  1978 *Language & Situation: Language Varieties & their Social Contexts.* London: Routledge.

Joos, M.
  1961 *The Five Clocks.* NY: Harcourt.

McEdwards, M.
  1968 *Introduction to Style.* Dickenson Publ. Co.

Roach, P.
  1983 *English Phonetics & Phonology: A Practical Course.* Cambridge: Camb. Univ. Press.

Wardhaugh, R.
  1976 *The Contexts of Language.* Boston: Newbury House

Speaker 1/Interpreter A

(That's why it's stay-has been around for so long / because it
has stayed / within the community // and it's been sheltered)

1.   'd like to talk a little bit about // the way deaf and

     hearing children learn language ///////

2.   now the typical American hearing child // learns English

     growing up ///////////

3.   when they're born //// even though they can't use the

     language overtly // parents will talk to them / using baby

     talk or whatever even / though the child may not understand

     at that point /

4.   they will continuely expose / the child / to spoken English /

5.   plus there will be other family me-members extended family

     and friends who will talk to the baby play with the baby and

     expose the baby to English ///////

6.   (cough) in addition there's um the media like tv and

     radio // which also provide additional auditory input //////

7.   andthen the child develops // the knowledge of the rules //

     and the grammar of the language /// intonation patterns //

um how to express their feelings and how to use the language

in different functions /////

8.   and that's just the natural acquisition process for a

hearing child ///

9.   now when a deaf child ////// if they have deaf parents //

the deaf parents will use ASL with them all the time //

10.   same way that a hearing child communicates with the hearing

parents ////

11.   and the child will get to know // ASL's rules ///// know how to

show their emotions know how to use ASL in different

situations

12.   so really they're :very very: parallel ////////

13.   now those children who learn ASL from their parents :and

have this first language as their native language: / they

tend to do better // in terms of learning English :and they

tend to be more skilled at English as a second language

because they already have: a first language

as a base /////////

14.   now this other group // of people that we're talking about

S1/IA

// are // deaf children who are born to hearing parents and
that's about ninety percent of the deaf population / who
are born to hearing parents //

15. a-nd they usually do not know ASL // and so there's alot of
communication difficulties and problems //

16. and many parents do not know how to deal with deafness ///

17. and so they continue to try to expose the child to language
and they will continue to use :spoken English with the child
even though the child cannot receive any of that input: ///

18. and their(?) / extended family and friends and they'll put the
radio on and tv /just like // as if their child were hearing /////

19. and so the child who's relying totally on the eyes is
not getting the language that the parents think that they're
giving them //////

(so they do not develop the rules and the grammar and how
to express themselves in that language in different
situations)

Speaker 1/Interpreter B

(Those are three reasons that ASL has <u>managed</u> under such difficult circumstances to survive through the years)

1.   I'd like to talk now about /// deaf and hearing children //

2.   and how they / learn language and :make a comparison between

the two: ///

3.   first let's talk about hearing children of hearing parents

here in America for example //

4.   they speak English //

5.   the parents // :speak English :and they bear a child and

that child /// as the child grows // the parent-s talk /

whether the child understands or not

6.   they continue to contto speak //

7.   they //// may the the baby may or may not understand may

look at them and not understand a word

8.   but the parents the aunts the uncles the cousins the

brothers sisters friends // everyone comes and talks at

that baby //

9.   the child is constantly bombarded with English as / he or

she grows //

10. tv // radio and a variety of media /// are constantly

bombarding that child 'til that child learns English

learns it's rules / learns how to combine words and /// how

to use inflection how to show emotion /////////

11. how to how to structure things like questions statements and

commands

12. ya know // all the inner workings of the English language//

13. now let's compare that to a deaf child born of deaf parents ///

14. deaf parents sign ASL to that deaf child in the very same

way day-n all day long // very same way that hearing parents

s-peak to their deaf to their deaf :to their hearing child: ///

15. :so therefore a child who is deaf of deaf parents grows up

learning the rules / gets comfortable with the language: ///

in exactly the same way that an English speaking child

learns English from hearing parents //

16. and their language is good //

17. their first language /// is / :they have excellent first

language skills and they can transfer those language skills

S1/IB

```
          f                              f
to their second language when they learn English
         f                        F
18.  they tend to to learn English more easily: //
                            f r
19.  :now let's look at the third case: //
        f   r              f   F
20.  hearing parents who have / a deaf child /////////////
       r              r             f
21.  you know out of all the deaf children born in the United
      f                                     F
     States :out of all the deaf children born period ninety
      f-r                          F
     percent: are born to hearing parents //
                   f      r                              F
22.  now when that occurs there's a g-reat deal of dis-com-fort
                             F          f-r             f
23.  hearing parents often know nothing a-about how to // teach
       f      f                        F
     a / a deaf child or what to do about a deaf child /
                    f            r                          f
24.  they will continue to talk just as they would to a hearing
      r                                      f-r
     baby /// :even though the deaf child can't hear:
      r         r               r            f          f
25.  friends // relatives :and so forth will come over and talk
      f    f    F
     at that child: //
            f-r                          f
26.  tv and radio will continue to be played but because the ears
         f-r                    F
     are closed / the deaf child is not getting the language
      r
     input //
```

(so the deaf child grows up with no sense of language
developemen-t when they get to be five or six years old and
go into school typically the deaf child doesn't know English
but doesn't know ASL either.)

Speaker 2/Interpreter A

(no preceeding utterance-begin at beginning of the tape)

1. Well // after the birth of my son / now comes the
   interesting part /

2. I wanna talk 'bout about my experiences raising my son //

3. now my son's name is Larwan //

4. now :my name's Larry my wife's name is Wanda so we took the
   first halves of our two names and put 'em together: //

5. and we got Larwan ///

6. now my wife decided not // to work the first year after
   thebaby was born // and then we talked about what should we
   do //

7. ya know :sh-is my wife gonna continue to stay home: and / do
   the mother role and I'm gonna continue to work /

8. well we talked it through and we decided why not reverse roles ////

9. so / when my son was fourteen months old // my wife went to
   work and/I decided // to stay at home /// to take care of my
   son

10. and lemme tell ya boy // ~what an experience~ ////

11. ahh I couldn't believe it

12. I mean wanna talk about being at home /// my routines at
     home and outdoors 'n shopping 'n doing all the
     different kinds of things that I've learned taking care
     of him ///////

13. tell ya my son has gave has given me alot of wonderfully
     interesting activities and headaches too /

14. and I'm really I-I'm amazed at mothers and how they can take
     care of not only one child but s-several children

15. I don't know how they do it //

16. well ya know my son is-a my st-son is s-deaf //

17. and he would-a try to communicate w-with me using these
     different gestures ///

18. and at first I :didn't understand him and I thought he was
     just making things up: //

19. but ya know // that's not true at all

20. he was really communicating

21. he really had these ideas //

S2/I_A

22. and he was copying / the-seeing signs that I had made //

23. I mean at fourteen months I mean he was just very very verbal
    and he'd // try to make these gross motor movements

24. and then later on // they would develop into precise signs

25. and then I could recognize ah-ha these were _really_ signs
    that _he_ was trying to communicate to me ////

26. I have a / very large house / and alot of _rooms_ and // boy I
    had to really childproof that house

27. I mean I had to _watch_ him ///

28. :I almost wanted to put him on a leash to keep control of
    him 'cause he was all over the place: /////

29. now changing diapers ya know that wasn't a problem //

30. at first / I mean it was ¯really /

31. :I didn't know how to do it¯ right

32. I ohp: took off the diaper and what happened
    ¯he :urinated right in my face:¯ //

33. so // :that was the first and last time

34. now I know ¯as soon as I move the diaper¯ and I watch his
    face / and he makes a facial expression ¯just when he's

S2/IA

ready to go to the bathroom so I protect myself: ̄ //

35. so it was really funny I kinda watched his little games when

he does this ///

(washing clothes is one of my favorite things to do to)

Speaker 2/InterpreterB

'(no preceeding utterance-begin at beginning of the tape)

1. What I wanna talk about now is my experiences with my son //

2. my son's name is Larwan //

3. :my name's Larry //

4. my wife's name is Wanda /

5. we took half of each of our names put it together and make

    Larwan: ////

6. my wife stayed home after the birth of our baby and / and

    took care of him for a year while I worked /

7. and then we talked about :should we exchange roles should I

    stay home what should we do and should my wife go back to

    work: //

8. so we said hey why don't I stay home and / my wife go back

    to work /

9. and we agreed to do that

10. we had-t :really good communication and cooperation: /

11. well Larwah // when he was fourteen mon-ths old // my wife

    went back to work and I took over the ch-care taking of our

S2/IB

child //

12. and it was n-o-t easy let me tell you

13. I went through some really tough times //

14. there are four things I'm gonna talk about /

15. the things I do at home // what I do shopping / the out of

doors / and our routines //

16. those fours things are the things I'd like to talk about as

a housefather //

17. when I stay at home // Larwan gives / does so many

:wonderful ~activities and he's so active~: and / gives me

alot of headaches too

18. I think mothers are just fabulous who stay at home and have

three four different kids you know ///

19. communication is one important thing to talk about

20. my son Larwan is deaf //

21. and so we sign to each other

22. but sometimes I think he makes up the signs

23. ya know he uses really / weird signs ///

S2/IB

24. but then it turns out that the signs are purposeful ya know

and they're not off the wall //

25. so I have to watch real carefully and pretty soon I tune in

to what it was / that Larwan was saying //

26. and ya know it's funny I noticed that what he does is he's

so visual he picks up on everything that he'll watch what my

wife and I say and then he'll pick up on those things / and

use them himself

27. and they start out real gross and then they m-ove to really

refil-ned //

28. 's fascinating to watch the developement of those signs //

29. when we play we do so many things

30. we have in our house we have lots of rooms 'n //

31. it's a big house /

32. an-d a I have to really make sure that my house is childproof

33. :I feel like I need to walk around with him on a leash: //

34. but I don't

35. I want him to feel free ////

36. I'm fabulous for example at changing diapers

S2/IB

37. this is one of my skills //

38. when I first started I was a mess because he he pinched

     right into my face and :all those kinds of things

39. :but it happened one and only one time /

40. because now I know how to cover him up real fast: //

41. and :I can tell by looking at his facial expression whether

     I have to hurry or not: in covering up //

42. I / I think mothers do that

43. they learn / from their fa their baby's facial expressions

44. I guess I won't go into that any further //

(Washing clothes is another thing I've enjoyed)

VI. INTERPRETERS' RECOGNITION OF STRUCTURE & MEANING

Robert M. Ingram

Abstract

Interpreters as subjects performed three tasks, listening, simultaneous interpreting (spoken English to ASL), and transliterating (i.e. rendering spoken input into fingerspelled words or signs for words in the precise order of the original). After each task they completed two recognition tests—one for surface syntactic form and one for meaning. Results revealed a significant difference between interpreters working between a signed language and a spoken language and interpreters working between two spoken languages. The results have a bearing on reinforcement *vs.* interference in short term memory.

Definitions

Interpretation has traditionally been defined as a form of translating that "converts an oral message into another oral message" (Seleskovitch 1978: 2). It is distinguished from translation proper, in which the translator "converts a written text into another written text" (ibid.). This view, however, overlooks the possibility—as when deaf people are involved—that either language in an interpretation may be signed instead of spoken. It would therefore be more accurate to define interpretation as a (form of the translation) process whereby messages encoded as discourse in one natural language (source Lg) are recoded as discourse in another natural language (target Lg; see also Ingram 1985a, b).

99

Not all signed languages are natural languages; many deaf people in the United States and Canada use one or more of the various artificial systems that have been developed with the intention of giving visible glosses for English morphemes. These systems are known collectively as Manually Coded English (MCE). Similar coding systems for representing other languages are used in other countries. The dominant language of the majority of Americans born deaf, however, is not English, whether spoken, written, or signed; it is instead American Sign Language (ASL): "... clearly a separate language, distinct from the spoken language of the surrounding community" (Klima & Bellugi 1979: 2). It is also "a complexly structured language with a highly articulated grammar, a language that exhibits many of the fundamental properties linguists have posited for all languages" (1979: 4). These properties include topic-prominence, a varied array of aspectual markers, morphological distinctions between nouns and verbs, and special devices for deixis and anaphora.

Given that ASL is a natural language, it must follow that the conversion of a message out of English into ASL, or the reverse, meets the definition of interpretation offered above. On the other hand, the conversion of an English message into MCE, or the reverse, does not meet this definition. When a message is recoded or, more accurately, glossed by manual actions for spoken words (or letters), it has become customary (among sign language interpreters) to term the process *transliteration*. (Operating within a single language, transliteration would seem to have more in common with the process known as shadowing than with interpretation; this supposition will be taken up again below.)

Interpretation may be either simultaneous or consecutive. "In consecutive," says Seleskovitch:

the interpreter gives his interpretation after the speaker has finished his speech, which may last anywhere from a few seconds (a few dozen words) to several minutes (a few hundred or even a few thousand words). [But] simultaneous interpretation conveys a message into another language at virtually the same moment in time as it is expressed in the first language. The interpreter lags, at most, a few seconds behind the speaker. (1978:3)

To cognitive psychologists, simultaneous interpretation represents

... a complex form of human information processing involving the perception, storage, retrieval, transformation, and transmission of verbal information. Furthermore, linguistic, motivational, situational, and a host of other factors cannot be ignored. (Gerver 1976:167)

One factor that obviously plays a key role in simultaneous interpretation is memory. The information that an interpreter receives must first be processed through working memory, then short term memory. How much and what kind of information actually goes into, or can be retrieved from, long term memory is still an open question. Some interpreters claim that they can remember a great deal of the material they interpret, while others report that they remember very little.

We would like to know whether sign language interpreters can remember more after listening, after transliterating, or after interpreting, and we would like to know how they compare on these tasks with spoken language interpreters. We would also like to know what kind of information is remembered—form or meaning. Answers to these questions may help us to understand the complex process of simultaneous interpretation (of both signed and spoken languages), to construct more detailed and more accurate models of these processes, to develop better methods of training simultaneous interpreters, and to understand the similarities and differences in processing discourse by hearing and by sight.

Interpreting & memory

The subject of memory as a component of the process of simultaneous interpretation of signed languages has not been empirically studied. There have been studies, however, of memory in the interpretation of spoken languages. An early study by Barik (1969) failed to show any significant differences in recall scores after interpreting and after listening, but the range of values for each recall test was so small that Barik had to concede that his investigation was "much too cursory" and inconclusive. Gerver (1974) compared comprehension and recall scores of interpreters after listening, shadowing, and simultaneous interpreting. He hypothesized that his subjects, trainees nearing completion of an intensive course, would score lower after shadowing and interpreting than after listening, because of interference resulting from simultaneous listening and speaking. As for the difference between shadowing and interpreting, Gerver supposed that the additional processing required in interpreting might have either a blocking or a reinforcing effect.

The additional task of translating (interpreting) could either still further impair interpreters' ability to understand and retain what they hear, or the more complex analysis of the incoming message which is necessary in order to translate (interpret), rather than merely repeat it, would assist in comprehension and recall. (Gerver 1979:184)

Gerver's first hypothesis was confirmed; i.e. simultaneous listening and speaking (as in shadowing and interpreting) was found to deter comprehension: scores were lower after shadowing and interpreting than after listening.

On the difference in memory after shadowing and interpreting, Gerver found recall and comprehension lower after shadowing than after interpreting. He concluded:

...where a person has the experience that even experienced students of simultaneous interpreting have of simultaneous listening and speaking, the simultaneity of the function does not in itself hinder the performance of concurrent cognitive tasks, although it may place some limits on efficiency of performance. (Gerver 1979:184)

Lambert replicated Barik's and Gerver's recall studies, with the added condition of consecutive interpretation, and found "no significant difference between listening, consecutive interpretation, and simultaneous interpretation" (1983:69). Recall scores after shadowing were lower than after the other three conditions, but the difference was significant only when compared with listening and consecutive interpreting. Lambert also tested her subjects on recognition for form and meaning. In addition to a recall test, her subjects completed (1) a word, or lexical, recognition test; (2) a word order, or syntactic, recognition test; and (3) a content, or semantic, recognition test.

In a pioneering study of listeners' memory for language in connected discourse, Sachs showed that "recognition memory for the form of a sentence declines much more rapidly (over time) than recognition memory for meaning" (1967:442). In other words, listeners quickly discard the surface syntactic form of an utterance while retaining the underlying meaning. Lambert wanted to know whether the same is true of interpreters' memory. She found that her subjects scored highest on the meaning recognition test, next on the lexical recognition test, and lowest on the syntactic recognition test. Scores for lexical and syntactic recognition were not significantly affected by the task (i.e. listening, shadowing, interpreting simultaneously, or interpreting consecutively). Such was not the case, however, for semantic recognition scores.

> ... recognition scores following listening were significantly higher... than the scores obtained following consecutive interpretation. The consecutive scores were, in turn, significantly higher ... than those obtained following simultaneous interpretation ... which in turn were significantly higher than those obtained after shadowing. (Lambert 1983:85f)

Lambert discusses her results in terms of the depth–of–processing theory of memory developed by Craik and Lockhart (1972). She concludes that "it would appear that deeper processing of incoming material occurs during listening and consecutive interpretation followed by simultaneous interpretation and lastly by shadowing" (Lambert 1983:109).

To summarize, research on interpretation of spoken languages has found that interpreters remember content much better than form, and that interpreters' ability to recognize content is impaired more by the task of shadowing than by simultaneous interpretation and more by simultaneous interpretation than by consecutive interpretation. The question remains whether the same distinctions exist for interpreters of signed languages. The experiment described below examined this question.

The hypotheses

1. Recognition for meaning is better than recognition for surface structure form (i.e. syntax) under all three experimental conditions: listening, transliterating, interpreting;
2. Recognition for syntax is not significantly affected by the type of task performed;
3. Recognition for meaning (i.e. semantics) is better after listening than after interpreting and better after interpreting than after transliterating.

If we equate transliterating with shadowing, on the grounds that both processes involve reiteration of the original message unchanged, we see that these hypotheses are consistent with the findings of psycholinguists who have studied interpretation of spoken languages.

The subjects, two males and nine females, were professional sign language interpreters from California State University at Northridge, all of whom were certified by the Registry of Interpreters for the Deaf (RID), a national professional certifying body. All but one held the highest, Comprehensive Skills, Certificate (CSC) at the time of the experiment. The other held the Interpreting Certificate. All eleven were native signers; i.e. were children of deaf signing parents. They participated in the experiment voluntarily and without compensation.

Before beginning the experiment the subjects answered questions about how much they thought they remembered after transliterating and interpreting and how much they thought most other interpreters and the best interpreters remembered after interpreting. No clear pattern emerged from their answers, nor could their opinions about recall be correlated with quality of performance.

Three narratives deemed to be similar in length, style, and complexity were selected from a textbook used for teaching English as a second language (NCTE, 1973). One text was used for each of the three experimental conditions: for listening, "The Life of a Farmer" (1973: 78ff); for transliterating, "A Modern Dairy" (1973: 94ff); and for interpreting, "The Life of a Hunter" (1973: 61f). All three texts were unknown to all of the subjects.

The story presentations were not counterbalanced across experimental conditions, both because a larger number of subjects would have been needed and because the selection of the texts virtually eliminated that kind of bias. A post hoc analysis of the texts reveals that they are similar in the number of clauses contained in each. The transliteration text does contain a larger proportion of passive verbs, but the presence of passive constructions in a text has been shown not to be a significant factor in message comprehension and recall (Sachs 1967, Charrow & Charrow 1979a, b). The texts were recorded at the Brown University Language Laboratory under studio conditions to avoid any background noise and interference in the tapes.

Two tests of recognition memory were constructed for each of the three experimental stories. Each semantic recognition test contained eight multiple choice questions on the information in the story. There were four choices, only one correct, for each question; e.g. after interpreting "The Life of a Hunter," subjects had to circle the correct statement from the choices below:
  (a) Alatook's father cut up the seal with a big knife.
  (b) Alatook's mother cut up the seal with a big knife.
  (c) Alatook's sister cut up the seal with a big knife.
  (d) Alatook cut up the seal with a big knife.
Each syntactic recognition test contained eight multiple choice questions on the syntactic structure of selected sentences from the story. Again there were four choices, only one correct. E.g. after transliterating "A Modern Dairy," subjects had to circle the statement below that actually appeared verbatim in the text:
(a) Wheat is the main grain crop grown on Mr. Taylor's farm.
(b) Mr. Taylor grows mainly wheat on his farm for grain.

(c) The main grain crop grown on Mr. Taylor's farm is wheat.

(d) The main grain crop Mr. Taylor grows on his farm is wheat.

On both the semantic and the syntactic recognition tests, the order of the questions was varied so as not to correspond with the order in which the information occurred in the story.

Each subject used all three stories and took all six recognition tests in one session. The order of the stories, and so of the experimental conditions, was varied (LIT for 2 subjects, ITL for 2, TIL for 2, LTI for 2, TLI for 2, and ILT for the last one). After the presentation of each story each subject completed first the semantic (content) test and then the syntax (form) test for that story. (The order of the two tests could not be balanced across subjects because the syntax recognition test contained some of the answers to the semantic recognition test.)

Each subject was tested individually in a session lasting approximately 75 minutes. The instructions for the listening task were as follows:

Please put on the headphones. You will hear a tape of a story titled "The Life of a Farmer." Just listen to the story, and you will be asked some questions afterward. Ready?

The subject was then given the opportunity to adjust the headphones before the tape was played. After the tape the subject received the semantic recognition test with these instructions:

Each numbered item on your test sheet contains four statements (A, B, C, and D), each expressing a different idea. Using your answer sheet, please circle the letter of the statement which is most closely in accordance with the facts given in the story. If you are uncertain about an answer, please guess. Do not leave any items unanswered, and please do not mark on the test sheet. Ready? Begin.

Similar instructions were given for the other tasks and tests, and the subjects were told that their interpretations and transliterations would be videotaped. They were used to being videotaped, and performances did not seem to be affected by this condition. When all three tasks and tests were completed, the subjects were permitted to ask questions or discuss the experiment with the experimenter.

Table 1. Raw scores, means, S.D. & Mean %

Subject	Listening		Transliterating		Interpreting	
	Sem	Syn	Sem	Syn	Sem	Syn
1	6	4	7	5	8	5
2	7	5	7	2	8	1
3	7	4	8	6	8	2
4	4	1	7	1	7	1
5	7	4	7	3	8	4
6	7	4	8	5	7	4
7	4	3	8	3	8	1
8	7	3	7	4	7	5
9	8	4	7	3	8	4
10	4	4	6	5	8	3
11	7	5	8	6	8	8
Totals	68	41	80	43	85	38
Mean	6.18	3.72	7.27	3.91	7.73	3.45
SD	1.47	1.10	0.65	1.64	0.46	2.16
%	77	47	91	49	97	43

Table 2. Test score rankings by data type for each subject.

	Sem	Syn	Sem	Syn	Sem	Syn
1	4.0	1.0	5.0	2.5	6.0	2.5
2	4.5	3.0	4.5	2.0	6.0	1.0
3	4.0	2.0	5.5	3.0	5.5	1.0
4	4.0	2.0	5.5	2.0	5.5	2.0
5	4.5	2.5	4.5	1.0	6.0	2.5
6	4.5	1.5	6.0	3.0	4.5	1.5
7	4.0	2.5	5.5	2.5	5.0	1.0
8	5.0	1.0	5.0	2.0	5.0	3.0
9	5.5	2.5	4.0	1.0	5.5	2.5
10	2.5	2.5	5.0	4.0	6.0	2.5
11	3.0	1.0	5.0	2.0	5.0	5.0
Totals	45.5	21.5	55.5	25.0	60.5	23.0

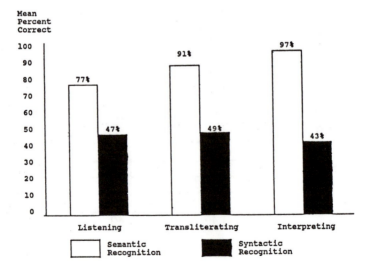

Figure 1. Mean percentage scores of 11 Subjects on 6 tests.

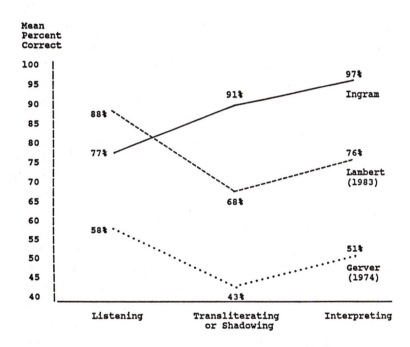

Figure 2. Comparison of mean percentage scores on semantic
memory   tests   across   three   experiments.

Results

Table 1 shows the raw scores (number of correct responses out of eight questions), and statistical results for all eleven subjects on all six tests. (Figure 1 below summarizes the results graphically.) The data were analyzed with the Friedman Test for Several Related Samples, a nonparametric test that employs ranks (Conover 1980). Each subject's scores on the six tests were ranked from lowest to highest (1 to 6 respectively), with ties receiving average ranks (Table 2). Each subject was ranked separately. The test statistic, F, has the value of 3.41 and is significant ($p \leq 0.01$; $d.f. + 5, 50$). This value indicates that the test scores for the six test conditions are not all the same. Pairwise comparisons of test conditions were made by comparing the difference between the rank sums for each test condition with a critical value.

Each of the semantic tests is significantly better than each of the syntactic tests ($p \geq 0.01$); thus Hypothesis 1 is confirmed. Among the syntactic tests no treatments are significantly different, confirming Hypothesis 2. Within the semantic tests, the transliteration and the interpretation tests are significantly better than the listening tests ($p \leq 0.05$ and 0.01, respectively), but there is no significant difference between tests for semantic recognition after interpreting and transliterating tasks. Thus Hypothesis 3 is not confirmed; semantic recognition is weaker after listening than after either transliteration or interpretation.

Hypothesis 1 predicts that recognition for meaning will be better than recognition for form under all three experimental conditions, listening, transliterating, and interpreting. The results confirm this hypothesis, and they demonstrate that at least in one respect, the priority of meaning over form in recognition memory, signed language interpretation does not differ from spoken language interpretation (Lambert 1983) nor from passive listening (Sachs 1967).

Hypothesis 2 predicts that recognition for syntax will not be significantly affected by the type of task performed; i.e. recognition of syntax after listening will be no less and no greater than recognition of syntax after interpreting or after transliterating. Confirmation of this hypothesis by this experiment demonstrates another similarity between signed language interpretation and spoken interpretation.

Hypothesis 3 predicts that semantic recognition tests will reveal a stepwise recognition, the greatest after listening, less after interpreting, and least after transliterating. Confirmation would have established a third parallel between signed and spoken language interpreting. The resulting non-confirmation suggests that there is a significant difference between signed language interpreting and transliterating.

Figure 2 shows a comparison (of mean percentage scores) on semantic memory across three experiments, the one here reported on signed language interpretation and two using spoken language interpreters as subjects: Gerver's recall study and Lambert's recognition study. The visual representation in Figure 2 shows clearly the difference between semantic memory after signed language interpreting and after spoken language interpreting.

What would explain this? The answer seems to be the difference in the mode of expression used by the interpreter. At least some types of memory are apparently modality specific (Kosslyn 1975, Paivio 1971, Shepard & Chipman 1971, Shepard et al. 1975) and limited in storage capacity (Baddeley & Hitch 1974, Baddeley et al. 1975). Brooks (1968) has shown that subjects performing complex cognitive tasks are able to respond ". . . faster in the conditions which would not be expected to compete for the same capacity, and slower when the task and response were within the same domain" (Klatzky 1980:165). In other words, an interpreter working from one spoken language to another should respond slower and presumably remember less than an interpreter working from a spoken language to a signed language, because two spoken languages would be expected to compete for the same limited storage capacity of short–term memory; while one signed language and one spoken language would not. In fact, the difference in modality apparently reinforces the underlying message, perhaps in the same way that taking notes during consecutive (not simultaneous) interpretation seems to reinforce recognition memory (Lambert 1983). Consequently, interpreters working in the same modality remember less after interpreting than after listening.

This explanation could be tested by requiring subjects to interpret from a signed language into a spoken language (e.g. ASL to English) and from one signed language to another (e.g. ASL to LSF, *langage des signes Français*). Such a modality–specific theory does not contradict the depth-of-processing theory advanced by Lambert for interpretation between two spoken languages.

Earlier in this study, I made the assumption that transliteration is a form of shadowing, because both processes involve reiteration of a message in the same language in which it is received—the only difference being that in transliteration the output is in a different modality. The results of the present experiment, however, argue against this assumption: no significant difference in semantic recognition was found whether the test followed transliterating or interpreting. This suggests that transliteration is not simply a programmed sensori-motor task but a task like interpretation that involves complex and deep cognitive processing—at least for the subjects tested here.

Betty Colonomos (personal communication) has argued that there are actually two types of trans-literation: processed and non processed. The latter is simply a matter of matching a sign to an English word, not to a concept. Processed transliteration, on the other hand, involves the matching of signs to concepts; the transliterator must concentrate on differences of lexical semantics, if not syntactic structure. (See Ingram 1985a, b, for more on the Colonomos models.)

All of the subjects in the present experiment, when asked to transliterate, used a variety of signed language more like Pidgin Sign English (see also Cokely 1983) than like manually coded English (i.e. close adherence to published manual codes for English words and morphemes). They used, in Colonomos's terms, processed transliteration. It might be revealing to test a group of transliterators using MCE (as non processed transliteration) to see how their scores on a semantic recognition test would compare with the scores of the group using processed transliteration.

The results of the present experiment need to be interpreted cautiously. In the first place the number of subjects tested is very small. Second, the experimental conditions were artificial: ambient noise was eliminated in the stimulus materials; materials were presented at moderate, controlled speed; and the materials were narratives only, not a variety of discourse types; interpretation was one way, from speech to sign and not the reverse. Further experiments should be conducted to determine effects of these and other variables on interpreters' recognition test performance.

These considerations notwithstanding, the experiment does present some evidence for the argument that there is a significant difference between the processing in signed language interpretation and the processing in spoken language interpretation, and that the explanation for this difference may lie in the requisite transfer to another modality.

REFERENCES

Baddeley, A. & G. Hitch
    1974   Working memory. In *The Psychology of
            Learning & Motivation*, Vol. 8, Bower ed.
            NY: Academic Press.
Baddeley, A., S. Grant, E. Wight & N. Thompson
    1975   Imagery & visual working memory. In
            Attention & Performance, Vol. 5, Rabbitt &
            Dornic eds. NY: Academic Press.
[Barik, H.
    1969   A study of simultaneous interpretation.
            Unpublished doctoral dissertation. UNC.]
Brooks, L.
    1968   Spatial & verbal components of the act of
            recall, *Canadian Journal of Psychology*
            22, 349–368.
Cokely, D.
    1983   When is a pidgin not a pidgin? An alter-
            nate analysis of the ASL–English contact
            situation, *Sign Language Studies* 38,
            1–24.
Conover, W.
    1980   *Practical Nonparametric Statistics.* NY:
            Wiley.
Craik, F. & R. Lockhart
    1972   Levels of processing: A framework for
            memory research, *Journal of Verbal
            Learning & Verbal Behavoir* 11, 671–684.
Gerver, D.
    1974   Simultaneous listening & speaking &
            retention of prose, *Quarterly Journal of
            Experimental Psychology* 26, 337342.
    1976   Empirical studies of simultaneous interpre-
            tation. In *Translation: Applications &
            Research* , Brislin ed. NY: Gardner Press.

[Ingram, R.
   1985a   Recognition memory among sign
           language interpreters. Unpublished
           masters thesis. Brown University.]
   1985b   Simultaneous interpretation of sign
           languages: Semiotic & psycholinguistic
           perspectives, *Multilingual Matters*
           4, 91–102.
Klatzky, R.
   1980   *Human Memory: Structures & Processes.*
           San Francisco: Freeman.
Klima, E. & U. Bellugi
   1979   *The Signs of Language.* Cambridge, MA:
           Harvard University Press.
Kosslyn, S.
   1975   Information representation in visual
           images, *Cognitive Psychology* 7,
           341–370.
[Lambert, S.
   1983   Recall & recognition among conference
           interpreters. Unpublished doctoral disser-
           tation. University of Stirling.]
NCTE
   1973   *English for Today; Book Three: The Way
           We Live.* 2nd ed. New York: McGraw Hill.
Paivio, A.
   1971   *Imagery & Verbal Processes.* NY: Holt, R.
           & Winston.
Sachs, J.
   1967   Recognition memory for syntactic &
           semantic aspects of connected discourse,
           Perception & Psychophysics 2, 437–442.
Seleskovitch, D.
   1978   *Interpreting for International Conferences.*
           Washington, DC: Pen & Booth.

Shepard, R. & S. Chipman
  1971   Second-order isomorphism of internal
          representations: Shapes of states,
          Cognitive Psychology 1, 1–17.
Shepard, R., D. Kilpatric & J. Cunningham
  1975   The internal representation of numbers,
          Cognitive Psychology 7, 82-138.

Note. The author thanks Brown University Graduate School for the grant supporting the research reported here and in his master's thesis. He thanks as well all those who assisted him in the project, and especially the interpreters at California State University, Northridge, who participated in the experiment.

VII. Miscommunication in Interpreted Classroom Interaction

Kristen Johnson

Abstract

Miscommunication or confusion can and does occur between deaf and hearing people when using sign language interpreters in university classrooms. In order to examine this I videotaped thirty–two hours of class-room sessions and with the help of colleagues transcribed and analyzed the spoken and signed language utterances for discrepancies between what was said by the hearing members of each class and what was transmitted to and understood by the deaf student. I found that numerous misunderstandings led directly to confusion on the part of the deaf student. These instances of confusion occurred with the greatest frequency when interpreters were unfamiliar with the subject they were interpreting and/or were required to interpret diagrams or verbal descriptions. The data also showed that the deaf students experienced difficulty looking at the board and at the interpreter simultaneously. In this paper I examine these two problem areas in depth and suggest strategies for reducing miscommunication in university classes.

Interpreted classroom communication

I set out to study the kinds of miscommunication that can occur between hearing and deaf people in university classrooms when an interpreter is used. In recent years, a number of scholars (Gumperz & Tannen 1979, Gumperz

1982a, 1982b, Gumperz & Cook–Gumperz 1982, Scollon & Scollon 1981, Phillips 1974, Dumont 1972, and Goffman 1981) have stressed the need to view language as only one aspect of communication. These studies focus on language as embedded in a social context and consider the ways of speaking and the rules for language variation as largely unconscious; i.e. out of the speaker's control. It becomes the task of ethnographers to explore the cultural patterns of behavior, perceptions, and attitudes that are learned and used in everyday interaction.

Similarly, the literature on deaf studies (Baker 1976, 1977, Baker & Cokely 1980, 1981, LeMaster 1986, Bellugi 1986, Bellugi & Klima 1975; Bellugi et al. 1988, Bihrle et al. 1988, Klima et al. 1979, Lillo–Martin et al. 1983, 1985, Mather 1987, Padden 1980, Padden & Humphries 1988, Rasmus & Allen 1988, Stokoe 1970, Woodward 1972, 1973, 1982, Johnson & Erting 1984) treats of various topics (e.g. conversational regulators, spatial relationships in sign language, development of complex signs, and Deaf ethnicity) that help us understand not only American Sign Language (ASL) and Deaf culture but also their cultural implications in hearing and deaf people's interactions.

Additionally, work on sign language interpreting by Cokely (1984) and Cannon (1980) draws our attention to certain aspects of interpreters' experiences and miscues. Both bodies of literature—sign language interpreting and deaf studies—enable us to understand Deaf people's experiences and what it means to communicate through a third party.

The present study approaches American Deaf culture in the same way an anthropological researcher would approach the study of a Samoan culture, an Indian tribe, or people from Indonesia. It recognizes the cultural uniqueness of Deaf Americans, and treats their traditions and norms as worthy of study and respect. It is an attempt to understand the root causes of the daily frustrations deaf students experience when interacting with a culturally different majority in hearing American classrooms. Secondly, it looks at the effect of the presence of a third party, the interpreter acting as intermediary, and at the consequent increase in

miscommunication over what would otherwise occur
between two interlocutors with different linguistic and
cultural backgrounds.

When I first began this study, I was relatively unaware of
the extent to which mis-communi-cations occurred in
hearing–deaf interactions via an interpreter. As a Deaf
student, I was aware that I frequently left my classes feeling
confused. But I often had little idea of what I was confused
about. Only after a few interpreters had discussed with me
the various problems in interpreting did I consider that the
source of confusion might not lie entirely within me. When I
began videotaping one of my classes, to my surprise I found
numerous instances of miscommunication upon viewing the
tape—this was the initiation of this project.

Definition & Hypothesis

It is well documented that signers often switch back and forth
between varieties of ASL and varieties of English. This
switching has been described as an example of bilingual
diglossia (Stokoe 1970, Woodward 1973, Woodward &
Markowicz 1975, Markowicz & Woodward 1978), in which
the more English–like varieties are used for out-group
functions, specifically where Deaf people are interacting with
hearing people or non signers; while the more ASL–like
varieties, in contrast, are generally used for in–group
functions, particularly among all–Deaf groups (Johnson &
Erting 1984:2f). In a mainstreamed college classroom, where
hearing and Deaf persons mix, the more English-like varieties
ranging from Pidgin Signed English (PSE) to Manually
Coded English (MCE) are often used. ASL may be used, if
the interpreter is skilled enough to sign it and the Deaf student
expresses a preference for it. In the classroom sessions
analyzed here, however, the English–like variety is the
predominant mode of communication used by the
interpreters.

Given that: (a) English–like signs are often used in
mainstreamed university classrooms; (b) conversation in the

classroom between deaf students and hearing professors and other hearing students is primarily through the sign language interpreter; and (c) sign language interpreters must mediate between hearing and deaf individuals who use different languages, different conversation regulators, and different cultural norms—I hypothe-sized that confusion and miscommunication were likely to result.

To test this hypothesis I made videotapes of classes in which I as a member of the Deaf culture, used an interpreter to communicate with members of my class. I taped also other Deaf students' classes in which the primary mode of communication was also through the use of an interpreter. From these tapes it was possible to make an ethnographically informed analysis of hearing and Deaf communication in a classroom setting to see how each of the participants—Deaf students, hearing students, interpreters, and professors—in each class may have contributed to instances of mis-communication, and to what extent the participants and the interpreters were aware that mis-communi-cation had occurred.

I videotaped 32 hours of class time in eleven different classes on a large university campus in California, with a Minolta 8-8100 camcorder. Ten of the courses were graduate level, one an undergraduate upper division course. In all of the tapes the video camera focused upon the interpreter, the Deaf student, and the professor. Some hearing members of the classes were also included, so that their interaction in the discussion could be viewed. Seven different interpreters were involved. Two of the seven were fully certified, holding the Comprehensive Skills Certificate (CSC) from the Registry of Interpreters for the Deaf (RID). The other five held partial certification.

In addition to the interpreters, four different Deaf students were videotaped (one male, No. 1, and three females, Nos. 2, 3, 4). Only one of the four Deaf students was present in any given class. All of the Deaf students were above the age of 30. The male Deaf student was a doctoral candidate with no residual hearing. In the videotape, he spoke and signed for himself even though the sign language interpreter also voiced for him. Deaf student No. 2 was me, a graduate student in a master's degree program. I have known sign language for over ten years, and I am profoundly deaf. In the tapes, I spoke and signed for myself. Deaf student No. 3, a fluent signer with no residual hearing, has known sign language since she was five years old. She was in a Ph.D. program and the interpreter voiced for her. Student No. 4, a foreign Deaf student with no residual hearing, had resided in the United States for a little more than a year. She had a fair command of written English and American Sign Language, but had trouble lipreading and reading fingerspelling. The interpreter voiced for her.

The spoken language utterances of all members of each class (the professor, the hearing students, and the Deaf students) as well as the sign language used by the interpreter and the Deaf student were transcribed and analyzed for discrepancies. Because of the tremendous amount of data in the 32 hours of tape, full transcription (both voice and sign language) was not made of all the tapes. Instead, the tapes were screened by three different people: a doctoral student in applied linguistics, another doctoral student in linguistic anthropology, and myself, a graduate student in cultural anthropology. Both of the doctoral students working with me are also interpreters holding Comprehensive Skills Certificates (CSC) from the Registry of Interpreters for the Deaf (RID). Instead of randomly picking areas of the tape to screen for misunderstandings, we focused primarily on areas where there was interaction between the Deaf students and their professors. We screened the tapes for discrepancies in several ways: (1) We looked to see if the interpreters had interpreted parts of the professor's lecture correctly; e.g. we noted cases in which the interpreter missed a whole passage or sentence, misspelled a word, conveyed an incorrect concept, or used an inaccurate sign. (2) We documented all the cases in which we felt that the answers that either gave to the other were inappropriate. (3) We documented the parts where feedback from the interpreters in the tapes indicated they felt that they had not interpreted the professor's message in the best possible way. (4) We also selected parts of the tapes where I had felt confused when I was the participating Deaf student.

Although we documented all segments that we thought contained problems or sources of conflict, it was not until after the transcriptions were completed that the two most consistent problems emerged: interpreting diagrams and verbal descriptions, and the problem of visual shifting. This paper focuses on these two problems. (Samples of transcriptions and ethnographic information are included in the Appendix.)

The most consistent problems found in the data were of two categories: first, the difficulties interpreters encounter when interpreting drawings or verbal descriptions of drawings that professors use to illustrate their lectures; second, the difficulties Deaf students have in looking at the board, a videotape, or other visually presented materials while simultaneously trying to look at the interpreter. Both of these problems can contribute to a variety of confusions, as the transcriptions and the analysis below will show. While the problems overlap, I discuss them separately here to help in understanding both types of situations and the difficulties they present.

Interpreting diagrams & descriptions: Thai house

Two transcribed segments from two graduate anthropology seminars are analyzed below: (1) a description of a Thai house description; and (2) the Thai house revisited.

1. The Thai house. This segment begins with the description of a Thai house given by a professor in a graduate anthropology class. (See the transcript in the Appendix, beginning at line 2845.) There were three students in the class: two hearing students (Nicole and Ron) and myself (Kristen). The other participants were the professor and the sign language interpreter. The professor's description of the Thai house was spontaneous, occurring in the midst of a discussion of the his field work in Thailand. In other words, there were no prepared handouts or diagrams on the board showing a picture of a Thai house. Instead, the professor drew a rough sketch of a Thai house on the board at the same time he was verbally describing it. This section shows in detail the difficulties that the interpreter and I had in following and understanding the professor's description. Four examples of these interpreting difficulties were analyzed. I have identified them as: (a) platform with posts, (b) an after–cabin, (c) beams, and (d) shelves with water containers.

a. A platform with posts. The Thai house as described by the professor was built on a platform with posts (See Appendix for a picture of a Thai house). In the description (section 2886) of the house platform built on posts, the interpreter assumed that it was built on *four* posts (since the professor never specifically stated how many posts), so she signed PLATFORM with four posts. She signed spatially where the posts were in relation to the platform. The picture conveyed looked like this:

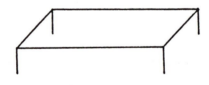

Figure 1

The interpreter did not know the size of the house on the platform, but she signed it as being a little smaller and in the middle of the platform, giving a picture like that below:

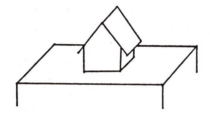

Figure 2

As these two examples illustrate, it is often unnecessary in English to specify how big something is, or exactly where an object is spatially located; but these two features are essential in Sign. In order to portray the spatial relationships accurately, the interpreter needed to know: (a) how many posts there were, (b) how big the platform was, (c) how big the house was in relation to the platform, and (d) where the house was located on the platform. This is an example of Scollon and Scollon's (1981) "content organization," which refers to the differences in the way talk is conceptually organized in languages, in this case in Sign and in English. The fact is that a visual language incorporates more information about what objects look like and how they are spatially related to one another than does English. This is a basis for miscommunication or confusion, as we shall see in further examples.

It is important to keep in mind that the picture the Deaf person ultimately receives is not necessarily the same as the one that the professor describes. Rather, it is what has been given to the Deaf person by the interpreter, because the Deaf person does not know what specifications the professor is giving in the description. For all the Deaf person knows, the professor could have actually said "four posts." Although the specifications could be conveyed through watching the interpreter's face (as the interpreter mouths or quietly shadows the professor's speech), sometimes the Deaf person does not or cannot lipread, or perhaps misses what was said on the lips at a given moment. At other times the interpreter's mouthing is not exactly as the professor said it.

The point is that the Deaf person is going to operate with the picture that is presented by the interpreter, which is necessarily based on whatever information is given by the speaker. If speakers do not give specific details needed for signing the concept, then interpreters must interpret and create them based on whatever information they do have, which is often a difficult task.

In this segment, confusion resulted not from the interpretation of the house on a platform with four posts but because the interpreter used three different signs for "platform" between segments 2886 and 2905. The drawings in Figure 3 show the differences in each of the signs. The first PLATFORM in segment 2886 might be taken for the sign AREA or SURROUNDINGS. The other two PLATFORM signs in segment 2906 differed from each other in that one used movement and the other did not. Because these last two used the same spatial format, they were not as confusing.

| Moved hand around | Did not move hands suggesting shape of platform | Moved hands l. to r. to show spatial outline of platform |

Figure 3

This progression of signs illustrates the interpreter's own initial confusion, which she gradually repaired. At first, the interpreter herself was unsure what the professor meant. It was not until the lecture went on and she gathered more information that the picture became clearer to her (Personal Communication from the interpreter). She therefore chose somewhat more accurate signs each time the word "platform" was mentioned in an attempt to repair previously unclear signs. Unfortunately, I was unaware of this and remained confused.

What is important to note here is that it was not just a miscue that caused the confusion. The professor was also unaware that the pace of his talk did not allow enough time for the interpreter (or me) to look at the board after each description. Scollon and Scollon's (1981) concept of "distribution of talk" which refers to the mutual agreement between individuals as to who talks first, holds the floor, how each takes a turn or interrupts is useful here as a means of locating an especially problematic aspect of discourse for Deaf students. The exchange between when the Professor talked and when the interpreter looked was not mutual. The interpreter was usually a couple of sentences behind the professor so that when she looked at the board, the professor had already pointed, made a comment, and moved on. As a result, she (and therefore I) became confused.

Phillips' (1974) and Dumont's (1972) work suggests that we are witnessing two different cultural norms here. Writing and talking simultaneously at the board is a cultural norm for hearing people. For Deaf people it is not. A Deaf professor would wait for the students to look before going on. As noted by LeMaster, hearing and Deaf people have "a different way of gaining access to communication. Deafness creates a reliance on visual access whereas the ability to hear leads to greatest reliance on the aural/oral channel of communication" (1986:4).

b. An aftercabin. In segment 2905, the professor made the analogy that a Thai house is like a boat with a large front deck and small aftercabin, which is an excellent comparison in English. But in signs that follow the English word order, it can be very confusing, particularly with the sign BEHIND. No indexing was done, either in terms of where the front deck was nor where the small aftercabin was. The signs were more word–based than meaning–based (Rasmus & Allen 1988). Figure 4 illustrates what the signs portrayed. One example of confusion was that the interpreter signed "BEHIND C-A-B-I-N," indicating in Sign that there was something behind the cabin, but *aftercabin* means a cabin toward the rear of a vessel.

WITH LARGE FRONT D-E-C-K

SMALL BEHIND C-A-B-I-N AND

WITH 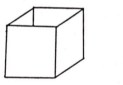   (4 WALLS) AND

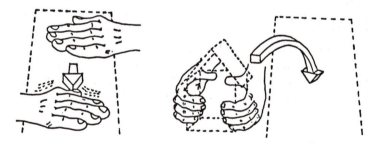

Figure 4.

What was even more confusing, and does not have to do with the signs themselves, is the sign AND between the description of the boat and the Thai house. There was no indication that the analogy was completed, and that the discussion was back on the Thai house. At the end of segment 2906, the interpreter noticed the confused look on my face and made a repair. She stopped interpreting and explained that the professor meant that the house was toward the back rather than exactly in the center of the platform. Although I responded with a nod, I was still not clear as to what the miscue had been. All I knew was that the interpreter had just made a repair. But the question remained, "A repair of what?" Was it a repair of her own signs, or was it an explanation specifically for me because I did not understand what had been said? I did not speak up nor ask any questions because I did not know specifically why I remained confused. As this example shows,

making repairs puts pressure on Deaf students to appear to understand even when they do not, and can create a conflict, because they may be unable to identify the cause of their confusion. If I had tried to understand my interpreter's repair, I might have missed what the professor said after that; or if I went ahead without trying to understand the nature of that particular repair, I might not have had the foundation to understand the rest of the Professor's descriptions. Now that I have analyzed this videotaped segment, I know what questions I could have asked the professor in order to clear up some of the confusion that I had. But at the time, I did not know that my confusion was caused by my lack of understanding of the interpreter's repair; I simply thought I did not understand the material.

   c. The beam. The most serious misunderstanding of the lecture occurred with the word *beam*. To review, the transcription at 2924 and 2925 reads as follows:

> *Professor*: Where the door is there's a um (. .) a (. .) a wooden um (. .) .I guess you don't call it a beam if it's (. .) if it's not in the ceiling (.) but (.) threshold I guess or something like that. It runs the length of the house (.) And on this side (. . .) is where people sleep (.)

gaze back, rt

Interpreter: WITH DOOR I-S . . . . . WOOD GUESS NAME B-E-A-M

ON B-E-A-M (rh) B-CL 'front-to-back' (1) ENTER LONG O-F

HOUSE G-CL 'narrow strip close-to-far' (2) ON THAT -rt S-I-D-E
    gaze back rt
WHERE PEOPLE SLEEP SLEEP IN

In this particular segment, the interpreter signed the first BEAM in a way that depicted the whole floor of the house. With the second BEAM it became a narrow strip running the length of the house (See Figure 5). Because the first BEAM was signed differently, and the second was not fingerspelled to indicate that it still referred to the same BEAM, I became even more confused. I knew only that there was a narrow strip of something. The fact that the second sign was a repair of the first sign was not made clear to me. In the next related segment, from 3069 to 3071, the professor came back to the idea of the beam. This time he explained that to cross over the beam was a serious offense. The interpreter signed, NOT ALLOW TO-CROSS-OVER THAT (2h)t C|-CL <—> 'BEAM' B-E-A-M ON FLOOR. This BEAM was signed at a 90 degree angle to the line of movement in the previous signs, and indicated a much wider BEAM than the second sign had. The drawings below illustrate the images projected by the three signs the interpreter used for BEAM.

At 3102, when I asked the professor about the beam, I wanted him to clarify where the beam was, and how it was related spatially to the house. But the professor's reply at 3108 showed that he was preoccupied with his use of the word *beam* itself. He tried to explain to me that it was more of a threshold than a beam. He did not understand my question nor did I understand his answer, because I was confused about placement and his whole concern was about his word choice.

BEAM 1 whole floor   BEAM 2. narrow strip   BEAM 3. half of house

Figure 5.

The professor, the interpreter, and I were all communicating on different levels. The professor was oblivious to the confusion that I was experiencing. I in turn did not realize that he was concerned with his word choice because of my own focus on the beam's placement and my frustration at remaining in the dark. Since the interpreter was also confused about how to sign the word *beam* in relation to the house, she was more concerned with trying to understand the description herself and finding a way to portray it for me, rather than conveying the actual footing[1] of the professor's

---

[1] "Footing" is defined by Goffman (1981:128) as "the alignment we take up to ourselves and the others present as expressed in the way we manage the production or reception of an utterance." This study expands on two of Goffman's meanings for this term. They are: (1) participants' posture or uprojected self," and (2) composition of the parties to the interaction. The first component (or meaning) of "footing" is the degree to which a speaker distances oneself from what is being said (or done), or from being the kind of person who says (or does) such things. In other words, the speaker is stepping aside from the statement to give it a different meaning; e.g. you can say something in such a manner as to question it, or to mark it as a quotation. You can convey respect or disrespect for the person you are quoting. "Footing" is a way of making

intonation when he expressed his concern about his lexical choice. Since this footing cue was not made clear, and each one of us was communicating on a different level, misunderstanding resulted between the professor and me.

In segment 3109 the interpreter signed BOARD LONG WOOD CENTER B-E-A-M TOP. The spatial relation-ship between the board and the middle beam was left unspecified. By this time the interpreter had resorted to a word-based transmission of the message, merely giving signs for the professor's words without even attempting to spatialize them. I was, consequently, left to wonder where *middle*, *beam*, and *top* were and how they were related to one another.

The interpreter realized this, and by the end of the professor's description finally understood what it was he was describing; so she once again attempted a repair for me on her own by signing a beam in the ceiling (right hand) and a flat wooden board paralleling it underneath (left hand) simultaneously. Because the spatial relationship was finally shown, I responded to the interpreter (not to the professor who was still talking) with, "Oh; Oh.""

d. Shelves with water containers. At segment 3000, the professor described a roof with shelves (interpreter: S-H-E-L-V-E-S) with water containers. Not knowing how big or

---

and changing one's posture or projected self, verbally and nonverbally. The second component of "footing" is the composition of the parties to the interaction. Goffman says that the common distinction between speaker and hearer is oversimplified. Sometimes the listener, the official hearer, is not really listening, and other times the unofficial hearers--the (intentional) eavesdroppers or people who overhear (unintentional)--are listening. Sometimes confusion arises over who is being addressed or who the participants are. For example, in a university classroom most Deaf students will have an interpreter and a notetaker. They are present there as the Deaf person's "ears," but are not officially in the class. Nevertheless, they are seen as "participants." Additional non-linguistic aspects of "footing" can include posture, body shifts, gesture, stance, eye-gaze, facial expression, intonation, or attitude. For example, "My, don't we look nice today" can be said with a tone of sarcasm or with admiration. "Footing" makes use of language and paralanguage, but is not confined to them.

small the containers were, or how many there were, the interpreter signed CONTAINER three times and showed them each to be about twelve inches tall. In addition, she fingerspelled the word *shelves*, demon-strating nothing about the spatial relationship of the shelves to the roof. This is analogous to the situation described earlier about the four posts and platform. Since the positioning of the hands always implies a particular spatial relationship, it bears repeating that sign language used by interpreters in classroom settings tends to (and needs to) give more specific relationships than English normally does. In this situation pertaining to the shelves, the professor was no longer drawing, but using his chalk to point to various areas of his drawing on the board of the Thai house. The interpreter, unable to see in time where the professor pointed, and not receiving enough information to convey the information in Sign, was lost. She was unable to index where the shelves would be in reference to the roof of the house. As a result, I became confused once again.

Summary of Thai house description

In each of the examples above, locatives in signs were critical to projecting the image and thus to understanding the description of the Thai house. But because the signs used did not often show their spatial relations to the Thai house, confusion resulted. Had the interpreter known exactly how the objects related to each other spatially (i.e. understood the message), she would have been able to sign it more clearly. For the most part, she had to outguess the professor when he referred to the platform with posts, the aftercabin analogy, the beam, the shelves, and the water containers: How many? Where? How close? How big? This was an awkward situation for the interpreter, for she, as the "unofficial" participant had always to weigh the situation and judge when it was appropriate for her to ask questions for clarification, while remaining in her official role as an interpreter. Another critical factor was that the interpreter was often aware that I was not understanding, and thus she undertook the task of repairing her signs. As was mentioned before, each repair puts pressure on the Deaf student to understand even when she or he may not. Most importantly, ASL tends to require more specific information regarding spatial relationships than English normally does, thus making the interpreter's job more difficult.

2. The Thai house revisited

In a later seminar, I was asked to review my first videotape and discuss with my class the interpreting difficulties of the Thai house description. For the discussion I set up another video camera to record the class watching the segment and making comments on it. The same interpreter was present again, so she had to interpret the Thai house scene a second time from the videotape.

While viewing this second tape afterwards, I wondered if the interpreter had signed the Thai house description any clearer the second time around. Although the interpreter was careful to use one sign for *platform* consistently, and not to make the mistake of signing HOUSE BEHIND when the word *aftercabin* came up, the answer to the question of whether she interpreted more clearly is a hesitant, "not really." But why? One would think that the answer would have been a firm "yes," given that the interpreter now had a better understanding of what the Thai house looked like. Although there were fewer ambiguities in the individual signs, the overall presentation of those signs was again vague in terms of spatial relationships. The reason for this may be that the interpreter did not have the drawing on the board to refer to. A careful examination of the second tape showed four major problems: (a) more fingerspelled words, (b) problems imposed by English word order, (c) lack of facial component, and (d) time lag.

a. More fingerspelled words. Fingerspelling is often used instead of signs when the signer is referring to a name of a place, object, or person; when there is no sign for that word; when the interpreter does not know a sign for a word or does not know the specifics of what the speaker is trying to convey and therefore, cannot fill in the gaps that are necessary for English to be translated into Sign. In this second viewing, it became obvious, particularly after speaking with the interpreter, that this interpreter did not know the specifics of the picture the professor intended to convey. She still had only a general idea of what the Thai house looked like, and there was no longer any drawing on the board to refer to; so the information given by the professor's words was even less sufficient for translation into Sign. The interpreter reported that fingerspelling seemed to be the safest way out. In other words, she avoided setting up confusing spatial relationships by merely spelling English words and so not specifying any spatial relationships at all.

b. Problems imposed by English word order. The interpreter signed so that the signs followed normal English word order; but in word-for-word interpre-tations from one language to another, important information is bound to be lost. In segment 1011, the professor said "the aftercabin is the house with walls." The interpreter signed "A-F-T-E-R C-A-B-I-N BOX (repeats) TALLER-BOX HAVE W-A-L-L-S." First, confusion began with the professor's statement "house with walls." In American culture, "house with walls" is redundant. Since he was making an analogy, it is safe to assume that the expressions *house with walls* and *aftercabin* did not directly apply to the house he saw in Thailand. Rather he was making an analogy by comparing a ship's "aftercabin" as we know it in America with a house in Thailand. This message was confusing as interpreted. "House with walls" was confusing in its redundancy, but it was even more so when the interpreter signed it the second time in larger dimensions (TALLER-BOX), and then signed HAVE W-A-L-L-S.

The question became: "Why the discrepancy between the first and the second sign for walls? Why the repetition?" Was it because the professor repeated himself or added some additional information? Unfortunately, in this tape the rest of his verbal description was unintelligible, but a discussion of this with the interpreter cleared up some of the confusion. The interpreter said that she remembered trying to picture the Thai house in her head, and decided at that moment that the walls should be bigger. In essence, the interpreter was making a repair by her sign and fingerspelled word: HAVE W-A-L-L-S. Since the nature of this repair was not made clear, it could have resulted in confusion. But because I was watching the videotape, instead of watching her, I did not see her sign it and therefore, it did not present a problem. Nonetheless, the interpreter's failure to communicate that she, not the professor, was making a repair was similar to the earlier incident with signs for *platform.*

c. Lack of facial component. In ASL, facial expressions are used to convey grammatical information; however, when an interpreter is faced with interpreting in English word order and is mouthing the words, many of the ASL facial expressions are sacrificed. In this particular case, the interpreter was not only having to sign in the English grammatical format and mouth the words, she also turned to glance at the video for visual information, which decreased her use of facial expressions even more.

d. Time lag. The amount of time needed for a sign interpreter to take in what the speaker says, reconstruct the meaning in signs, and express it is known as time lag. Cokely (1984, 1992 & above) examined the correlation between time lag and miscues. He videotaped six interpreters interpreting a similar event. Of the six, he chose four for a closer study of their interpreting skills and miscues. In these four separate interpreters' performances, he discovered that certain minimum lag times made a significant difference in the amount of miscues committed. In general, he found that it was interpreters who had shorter time lags who were more prone to making errors.[2] In other words, interpreters who were approximately less than a sentence behind the speaker

---

[2] See Cokely 1992 for a detailed discussion of the kinds of miscues made by interpreters: omissions, substitutions, additions, intrusions, anomalies.

were more prone to make miscues than interpreters who were approximately more than a sentence behind. It was clear that longer time lag helped the interpreters to get a better feel for which signs to use and in which order to place them to convey most accurately the ideas expressed in English.

Cokely's discussion of time lag is pertinent to the "Thai House Revisited" segments, because if we look, for example, at segment 1011 we find that the interpreter was only a few words behind the professor. This may have been a contributing factor to making the signs in 1011 ("houses with walls...") confusing, and why the interpreter had to make a repair. One factor that must be kept in mind is that the interpreter had heard and interpreted the Thai House segment before, and may have been interpreting closely behind because she knew what followed. The important point to make is that facial expressions, time lag, knowledge of the speaker's intended meaning, knowledge of the subject matter, communicating to the deaf person that a repair is being made, fingerspelling, and the differences in content organization between English and ASL—all these are factors that contribute to miscues and miscommunication.

Visual limitations

This section will discuss the visual limitations that interpreters and deaf students experience in the classroom. This subject is closely related to, if not actually overlapping, the problems of interpreting diagrams and verbal descriptions. Nonetheless, it is an area that merits individual analysis. The term "limitations" here refers to the Deaf person's need to look at the board, a textbook, a videotape, a handout, or other visual materials and at the interpreter—all at the same time.

Interpreters usually try to stand next to the video monitor or screen when a tape or movie is being shown, in order to make the visual shifting back and forth between the image and the interpreter as easy as possible. Even so, the Deaf student is likely to miss some information. Looking at the interpreter, for example, momentarily cuts out what is occurring on the movie screen, or vice versa. Deaf students constantly need to weigh the situation, and then hope whichever place they choose to look at any given moment will be the most useful to their understanding.

Too often, hearing professors and students who are used to listening to lectures and looking at videotapes at the same time do not think about Deaf students' difficulties in the same situation. Before we can discuss the visual problems found in the two classroom settings, we need to understand how differing norms and perspectives play a part in interactions between deaf students and hearing students in university classrooms.

Deaf people rely primarily on visual cues, while hearing people rely primarily on auditory cues for communication. In the classroom, hearing students can look at exhibits or their papers and write notes without missing any information. From time to time, they will divert their gaze from their papers to look at the lecturer. Deaf people, on the other hand, will usually sit in the front row, and look almost continually at the interpreter. Should their eyes divert to the professor, to the window, or to their neighbors in class, it is likely that they will miss something the interpreter signs—and therefore what the professor is saying. If the professor is referring to a diagram, for instance, most hearing students will look up to the place on the diagram the professor is discussing. For the Deaf student, this is impossible for two reasons. First, the interpreter is usually a sentence or more behind, so that by the time the Deaf student looks up at the diagram, the professor has already moved on. Second, while the Deaf student looks at the diagram, the interpreter usually has had to keep on interpreting, so some of what has been said is likely to be lost.

In an all Deaf classroom, the presentation style is quite different. Deaf speakers will stand in front of the class to make sure that everyone can read their signs. If they are going to use a diagram or sketch something on the board, they will first point to the diagram or draw, then wait until everyone has had a chance to look at the exhibit before they resume signing. This is in contrast to the practice of hearing lecturers who not only point to the board and talk simultaneously but also may be talking as they face the board and turn their backs towards their audience.

Eye contact is not as crucial in a classroom of hearing students as it is for a deaf audience. This can be seen in a humorous deaf opening line. Instead of asking, "May I have your attention please?" a Deaf lecturer will ask "May I borrow your eyes please?" Awareness of these different cultural norms could lead to finding ways to resolve the problems deaf students encounter in predominantly hearing classrooms. Learning how other cultural groups are working to resolve similar problems in classroom settings may also be useful. For instance, current suggestions to resolve the conflicts between Native American students and White teachers in classroom settings involve using Indian teachers as models to learn what actually works best for the students (Mohatt & Erickson 1981).

The Thai house: Nicole's reaction

The following is taken from the first Thai house session and transcriptions of Nicole's reactions. In the first data segment there is an example of the lack of cultural awareness that most hearing people have concerning deaf people. In this segment, I was explaining to the professor why I chose one of Erving Goffman's books. I told him that one reason I had picked a particular book of Goffman's, *Presentation of Self in Everyday Life,* was that I had seen my classmate Nicole outside of class the day before, and she had told me that *The Presentation of Self* was a very good book. While I was explaining this, Nicole reacted nonverbally to my comment by jerking her head backwards and staring down at the table with her eyebrows furrowed together as if she did not agree with my version of what had occurred.

I discovered later that I had misunderstood Nicole and that was the reason she responded with surprise to my comment. I had also missed her nonverbal cue in class because I was watching my interpreter. This situation would have gone unnoticed had I not videotaped the class and later viewed

Nicole's reaction. This scenario portrays the problems Deaf students encounter, unless of course, the interpreter is able to notice and incorporate this extra feedback in the interpreting process. But what about the hearing participants? Are they aware of this limitation on visual input? To test this, I brought the videotape of that session to class. Both my professor and Nicole expressed surprise when I told them I had not seen Nicole's reaction. In the tape the professor incredulously asks, "You didn't see her?!" and Nicole remarks, "...interesting that you didn't see my reaction [because] it was such a big [nonverbal] movement."

Since Nicole was sitting right next to me, both she and the professor thought I must have seen her reaction. However, since I was focusing on the signing of the interpreter, I missed Nicole's nonverbal cues. The interpreting situation almost exclusively limits Deaf people's vision to the interpreter; therefore, they may miss other uses of visual cues in the classroom. Had I known or seen Nicole's nonverbal expression, the dynamics of the situation would have been different. The point here is that the hearing participants' lack of awareness of the Deaf student's limited visual input can and does change the dynamics of interactions, and it demonstrates the communicative differences between hearing and deaf people via the interpreter. Because hearing interlocutors and Deaf interlocutors rely on different environmental cues, a myriad of conflicts, confusions, and misunder-standings can occur, particularly when neither party is aware of this. Since the Deaf student must look at the interpreter, the interpreter becomes the single channel for all the visual and sound cues that must be conveyed to the Deaf student.

Goffman's book

Another incident involving a misunderstanding between my anthropology professor and me may further help clarify the problems of visual limitations. Prior to the class the professor had loaned me his copy of *The Presentation of Self* by Erving Goffman. The seminar consisted of Nicole, Ron, the professor, and myself. Our class began with the discussion of Goffman's book:

Professor. I think this whole issue I wanted to raise (.) now (...) that for me is one of the (.) um (...) reasons why I liked *The Presentation of Self* so much (...) Now one reason is it was the first Goffman I ever read (...) and (...) wow is it exciting (...) don't know, if I may borrow that if this is my copy (...) I don't know what kind of (...) It's always dangerous to loan someone your own reading copy cuz it's full of such (...) oh no, it doesn't have too much scribbling in it (unintelligible)

A hearing student. (laughter)

Deaf student. I've not been writing in it at all!

Prof. No (.) I did.

Deaf student. Oh (.) *you* did! (...) oh!

Prof I don't want to (...) um (...) oh (.) I see it's got these numbers so I must have notes written elsewhere in (...) response to it um (...)

As the transcript shows, the professor was talking about the danger of leaving *his* notes or scribbles in a book that he was lending to someone else, in this case, to me. The misunderstanding occurred on my part when I broke visual contact: I looked away from the interpreter to hand the borrowed book to my professor. I looked back only in time to see *"dangerous to loan someone your own reading copy cuz it's full of such (...) oh no, it doesn't have too much scribbling in it."* I automatically assumed that the professor was accusing me of writing in his book, and responded with "I have not been writing in it at all!" The professor changed his footing by responding, "No, I did." He was aware that I had taken him literally and therefore made the effort to repair his former statement.

With regard to intonation, it may be hypo-thetically accurate to suggest that if the interpreter had signed the appropriate footing, despite the fact that I looked away for a few seconds, I might have caught on. Unfortunately, there was no way of testing this as the professor was inadvertently blocking the camera's view of the interpreter when he got up to take the book from me. When the professor said it was, "always dangerous to loan someone your own reading copy," the hearing transcriber noted that there was a slight chuckle or teasing in his voice. In addition, when he said, "Oh, no, it doesn't have too much scribbling in it," the tone in his voice implied that he was poking fun at himself. These are instances of footing that had not been conveyed to me, whether it was because I looked away or because the interpreter did not foot my professor's intonation accurately. My response reflected the misunderstanding.

This example of miscommunication demon-strates that the main problem was not caused by what the professor said but rather how he said it. Scollon and Scollon say:

It is the discourse system which produces the greatest difficulty, not the grammar. It is the way ideas are put together into an argument, the way some ideas are selected for special emphasis, or the way emotional information about the ideas is presented that caused miscommunication. The grammatical system gives the message while the discourse system tells how to interpret the message. (S&S 1981)

This helps to explain the miscommunication described above. It also shows that interpreters need to mediate as well as interpret words, and especially need to be aware of and compensate for the visual limitations that Deaf students experience in the classroom.

Implications of visual limitations

The videotaped data shows that visual limitations play a role in distorting the communication that I videotaped in both anthropology classes. The interpreters and the Deaf students may experience feelings of interactional disharmony with the professor and rest of the class because they cannot follow the interpreted discourse and acquire needed information from the board or from nonverbal actions. This, in turn, has deeper implications for classroom interaction because it may reinforce certain negative stereotypes about Deaf people's ability as students, and may tarnish Deaf people's self–image.

Goffman's notion of the "presentation of self" (1959) is useful here: it explains the differences between how deaf people feel they are presenting themselves and how an instructor may see them. For instance, a professor may not understand why a Deaf student is asking questions about something he or she may not have understood in class. The professor, not understanding where the deaf student is coming from, may misjudge the Deaf student's intelligence, "listening" skills, and so on.

Additionally, Deaf people may not know that the information they received in class was inaccurate, or that they did not get all the information that was necessary. There may be times when they will wonder why they did not understand the materials when their hearing classmates did. Their interpreters may also experience frustration and stress, perhaps knowing miscommunication is occurring, but feeling that they cannot control it. This in turn may cause them to make even more miscues than they normally do. In other words, not only does this triad communication have a sociological and cultural impact, but it has psychological implications as well, far more than this paper can elaborate on.

Conclusion

I hypothesized that significant miscommunication through the use of an interpreter could be found in university classrooms between hearing and Deaf people. The data summarized in this paper have supported that hypothesis by illustrating various types of misunderstandings and the subsequent confusion that can occur, by examining naturally occurring interactions between deaf students and the hearing members of a class via an interpreter. The data have also raised the issues of what perspectives, norms, intonation patterns, facial expressions, and "footing" (Goffman 1981) are conscious rather than unconscious, and what the consequences of these are for all the participants in Deaf–hearing classroom interactions. More particularly, the data portray the confusion surrounding the interpretation of diagrams and the problems of visual limitations facing the deaf person in the classroom.

One of the greatest cultural differences pertinent to these miscommunications appears to be the differing emphases on the visual channel used by Deaf people and the auditory channel used by hearing people, as noted by LeMaster (1986). Hearing people who have not come into contact with many Deaf people are often unaware of the visual needs of the Deaf student. The visual versus auditory conflict was reflected in the data in the use of language, conversation regulators, norms, and perceptions by both the hearing and Deaf participants in the anthropology classes.

The English used in both classes was also often inadequate for expressing spatial relationships accurately in sign language. The interpreter in the anthropology classes was also unfamiliar with the subject she was interpreting. As a result of both problems, the interpreter had to sign to the best of her limited knowledge and information, or resort to fingerspelling or word–based signs. These interpreter tactics often resulted in miscommunication and confusion, because the interpreter would sometimes use several different signs (e.g. for "beam") before the concept became clearer to her.

She was also unable to communicate to the Deaf person that she had made a repair, or that her word-based signs and fingerspelled words did not show how things were conceptually or spatially related. It bears repeating that repair requires more work and additional responsibility on the part of the Deaf student because of the potential for confusion.

The use of conversation regulators by both groups was also at odds because of the visual vs. auditory mode of presenting and communicating information. The anthropology professor spoke, drew, and pointed to the board or to a transparency at the same time. I had trouble following these discussions because my interpreter was a sentence or so behind, making it impossible for me to look at the board and follow the interpreter simultaneously. Without the visual input, I received only the professor's words, not his meaning. Similarly, the interpreter experienced difficulty with the limits of vision, because she had to face me and try to look at the board simultaneously. If she did look away from me, I missed those important facial expressions that carry grammatical information in Sign, or the features needed to read visually a word she was mouthing, or both.

Differing cultural norms for accessing and expres-sing information were also a source of conflict in the anthropology classes. To talk and write on the board is a cultural norm for most hearing professors. They do it to save time and to keep the audience's attention. Usually they do it without thinking. For deaf people, this sort of behavior is uncomfortable, and perhaps even unthinkable. The first Thai house example, in particular, demonstrates a culminating series of confusions that finally led to the miscommunication between the professor and me. He was writing on the board, which I could not see. Because of our different cultural norms of expressing and accessing infor-mation, when I became confused about the placement of the "beam" in relation to the house, he was unaware of my needs as a deaf student and instead interpreted my confusion as having been caused by his lexical choice of the word *beam* instead of the object's location.

Misconceptions about the job of the interpreter are also involved. Interpreters do not merely sign English on the hands, nor are they experts (with a few exceptions) in the subject they are interpreting. Their job is tremendous: they must not only interpret from one language to another, but they must also express the correct "footing" of the various speakers. Cannon (1980) sums up the role of an interpreter well:

Being an interpreter requires such unlearnable traits as iron nerves, instant recall, total concentration, a combination of speed and accuracy, and a consciously induced schizophrenia—the ability to divide the mind into two linguistic wholes (quoting Seagrane, *Washington Post* 1975:6).

Remedies

This presentation of problems would not be complete without a discussion of possible solutions. One solution would be to prepare deaf students to cope with the various problems that can occur in classroom interaction, and even encourage them to get involved in studies of this kind so that we may learn more about our own interactions with hearing people when using an interpreter. It is important for Deaf students to realize that the confusion they are experiencing may not originate in limitations on their own abilities, but may arise in the process of interpretation itself or in the inevitable cross-cultural exchange. When this is understood, Deaf students may be more willing to speak up and to try to resolve the confusion rather than just assuming it is their fault and accepting it passively.

Providing interpreters with formal opportunities to improve their skills would also be helpful to all parties involved in the communication process. For example, research is being conducted at the Salk Institute on spatial relationships in ASL. As the results of these studies become available, it would be helpful to incorporate them into interpreter training programs so that future interpreters may become more skilled at establishing spatial relationships in their sign language performance.

Perhaps interpreters could be encouraged also to study not only for the present level of interpreter certification, but also to progress beyond certification by entering various fields and obtaining higher degrees in subject areas in which they may be interested in interpreting: e.g. biology, English, law, and so on. In this way, they would increase their personal knowledge base as well as their ability to interpret effectively in specialized fields.

Finally, like non–Indian teachers who are using Native American teachers as role models to help resolve their conflicts in the classroom setting (Mohatt & Erickson 1981), it would be helpful to encourage hearing teachers to observe Deaf teachers as models to acquire a better understanding of the cultural and logistical differences in effective educational communication with Deaf students.

This study has touched on only a few aspects of Deaf–hearing communication. It is important to note that not all differences—different cultures, conversation regulators, norms, and so on—constitute problems. We should study why some differences may be problematic and others may not. Based on the findings of this study, it is clear that additional naturalistic research is needed before we can truly understand the various levels of communication and miscommunication that actually occur between hearing and Deaf participants in university classrooms where an interpreter is used.

APPENDIX
1. The Thai house as described (and drawn) by the Anthropology Professor

The transcription conventions used to record all of the sign language (manual) portions in the videotapes are taken from Baker and Cokely (1980) with their permission. In addition to the manual portion (reproduced on the following pages), nonmanual portions such as the facial expressions and certain head movements of the interpreters and signers were transcribed. These nonmanual behaviors are recorded on a superscript line above the manual signals. The duration of each nonmanual signal is indicated by the length of the superscript line. Specific nonmanual signals are abbreviated, and are as follows (from Baker & Cokely, 1980 & Cokely, 1984):

q = yes–no question; consists minimally of a brow raise and a tilt of the head forward

wh–q = wh– question; consists minimally of a brow squint and a head tilt.

neg = negative; minimally, a brow squint & a slight head shake.

Other nonmanual behaviors function often as adverbs and adjectives, and are as follows (from Cokely, 1984):

cs = very close in time or space
th = without paying attention; carelessly
mm = normally; regular; as expected
puff cheeks = a lot; huge number of; large

Special thanks to Bev Cannon for doing the voice transcriptions, and to Bart Johnson for the illustrations.

3. Samples of data transcription

2925 (Interpreter): ONE DOOR WITH DOOR I-S <u>gaze back.rt</u> WOOD
GUESS NAME B-E-A-M ON B-E-A-M (rh) BI-CL 'front -to-back'
ENTER LONG O-F HOUSE G-CL 'narrow strip close-to far' ON <u>gaze back.rt</u>
THAT-rt- S-I-D-E WHERE PEOPLE SLEEP SLEEP IN

2940 (Kristen): What?..What..What..What'd you say about sleep?

2941 (Interpreter): THAT S-I-D-E WHERE PEOPLE SLEEP SLEEP HAVE <u>(Int. signs on her own accord)</u>
BEE N-E-T-S

2943 (Kristen): Oh (..) where?

2945 (Nicole): Where do people sleep?

2946 (Professor): They sleep in here.

2946 (Interpreter): <u>gaze back.rt</u> THAT INDEX-back.rt (to blackboard) <u>gaze back.rt</u>

2947 (Kristen): Oh. Over there (...) oh

2949 (Nicole): (laughter)

2950 (Interpreter): V-CL 'people-lying-in-a-row'+++

2951 (Kristen): I (...) I didn't know where! I'm looking at you and I'm
looking up (to Interpreter) I didn't know where it was! (laughter)

2953 (Professor): Um (..) and here's uh (...) a fireplace (..) inside the
house

2956 (Interpreter): (rh) HERE <u>gaze back.rt</u> FIRE PLACE IN+ HOUSE <u>gaze back.rt</u>

2959 (Professor): You enter the (..) the house compound (.) That is (.)
there's (...) there's a fence built around the whole compound (.)
Outside there's a front yard and a back yard or whatever you want to call it
(.) You enter the house compound (.) That is to say if you're outside the
house compound (...) I'm gonna call that space number one (...) and then
you come into the house compound (...) and that's space number two (.)
And then you come over to (..) the staircase (...) that goes up cuz you
remember (.) you know it's built about six feet off the ground Um (...) the
base of the staircase (..) is another social space (..) And (..)

2960 (Interpreter): ENTER HOUSE C-O-M-P-O-U-N-D (2h) 4-CL
'fence around the house' ALL FRONT Y-A-R-D B-A-C-K-Y-A-R-D <u>gaze back.rt</u>
ENTER HOUSE C-O-M-P-O-U-N-D SHOW OUT-cntr HOUSE C-O-M-P-
O-U-N-D NAME S-P-A-C-E NUMBER ONE THEN ENTER <u>gaze back.rt</u>
HOUSE   THAT S-P-A-C-E NUMBER TWO (Int. gets up and
walks to the side of the blackboard) THEN COME-TO-lf-to-cntr TO S-T-
A-I-R-C-A-S-E V-CL 'walk-up-the-stairs' 6 FEET O-F-F <u>gaze down.rt</u>
DIRT   BOTTOM S-T-A-I-R-C-A-S-E OTHER SOCIAL

S-P-A-C-E AND

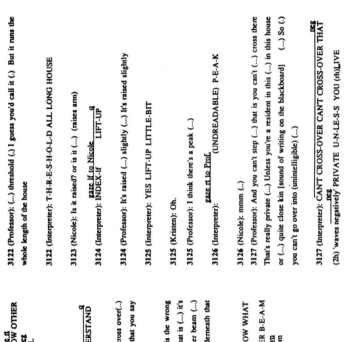

                          gaze rt
3089 (Interpreter): U-N-L-E-S-S BORN TOWN+ NOT ALLOW OTHER
     neg   neg
KIND ALLOW NOT ALLOW TO ENTER HOUSE #AT-ALL

3099 [sound of writing on the black board]

     [Int. signs to Kristen on her own accord]
                                              q
3101 (Interpreter):   UNDERSTAND

3108 (Kristen): (unintelligible) beam you're not supposed to cross over(...) (clears throat) (..) My voice (..) I lost it (..) What's the beam that you say that's not supposed to be crossed over?

3108 (Professor): Um (...) well (.) it's not like (...) a beam is the wrong word for it (.) I don't know what (...) what word to use (.) That is (...) it's sort of (...) It's a (...) It's a long house (.) And there's a center beam (...) up on the (.) you know (...) up on the top And directly underneath that center beam (...) is (...) um (...) a

                                                              gaze down
3109 (Interpreter): O-K B-E-A-M WRONG WORD NOT-KNOW WHAT
     gaze rt   gaze down
WORD   (2h) 1-CL outline 'board' LONG WOOD CENTER B-E-A-M
TOP AND INDEX-down (2b) G-CL '(lh)top beam, (rh) bottom
     gaze down rt
beam) <--->far-to-close'

3122 (Kristen): Oh. Oh.

3122 (Professor): (...) threshold (.) I guess you'd call it (.) But it runs the whole length of the house

3122 (Interpreter): T-H-R-E-S-H-O-L-D ALL LONG HOUSE

3123 (Nicole): Is it raised? or is it (...) (raises arm)
                    gaze lf to Nicole   q
3124 (Interpreter): INDEX-lf   LIFT-UP

3124 (Professor): It's raised (...) slightly (...) It's raised slightly

3125 (Interpreter): YES LIFT-UP LITTLE-BIT

3125 (Kristen): Oh.

3125 (Professor): I think there's a peak (...)
                    gaze rt to Prof.
3126 (Interpreter):   (UNDREADABLE) P-E-A-K

3126 (Nicole): mmm (..)

3127 (Professor): And you can't step (...) that is you can't (...) cross there That's really private (...) Unless you're a resident in this (...) in this house or (...) quite close kin [sound of writing on the blackboard]   (...) So (.) you can't go over into (unintelligible) (...)
                                                          neg
3127 (Interpreter): CANT CROSS-OVER CANT CROSS-OVER THAT
      neg
PRIVATE U-N-L-E-S-S YOU (rh)LIVE
(2h) 'waves negatively'

1930 (Professor): (...) you would have seen it (...)

1931 (Nicole): It was a big movement

1932 (Professor): That's really interesting

1932 (Nicole): That's really interesting.

1933 (Interpreter): THAT <u>V</u>ERY INTERESTING^{nods} THAT <u>V</u>ERY INTERESTING^{nods}

1933 (Kristen): Well (..)(laughter)

1934 (Nicole): What also I find interesting is that the (..) the misunderstanding we had about the book (...) I don't think that's necessarily even an artifact of (..) of (..) of deaf hearing miscommunication (...) I think that could be a miscommunication between anybody (...)

1934 (Interpreter): YES BUT WHAT^{gaze lf to Nicole} SAME+ I FIND INTERESTING THAT MISUNDERSTAND WE HAVE ABOUT BOOK I NOT THINK^{neg} MUST+ A-R-T-I-F-A-C-T O-F DEAF HEARING MISUNDERSTAND^{neg} THINK CAN B-E ANYONE-arc^{nods}

1938 (When the tape on the video monitor ended, the machine suddenly made a horrible, loud noise Nicole jumped, but Kristen oblivious to the sound, responded to the Nicole's comment simultaneously with the noise) I agree (.) Uh huh (.) I agree (.) I agree (.) Uh huh (.) Yeah (.) Uh huh

1940 (Nicole): But it's interesting that you didn't see my reaction

1940 (Interpreter): BUT INTERESTING THAT NOT SEE MY <u>R</u>ESPOND

REFERENCES

Baker, C.

1976   Eye–Openers in ASL, in Cal. *Linguistics Assn. Conference Proceedings*, San Diego State University.

1977   Regulators and turn-taking in ASL discourse. In *On the Other Hand: New Perspectives on American Sign Language.* NY: Academic Press. 215-236.

- - - - - & D. Cokely

1980   *American Sign Language: A Teacher's Resource Text on Grammar & Culture.* Silver Spring, MD: T.J. Publishers. [Gall. U. Press,1991]

1981   *American Sign Language: A Student Text, Units 10-18.* Silver Spring, MD: T.J. Publishers. [Gall. U. Press 1991]

Bellugi, U.

1986   The Acquisition of a spatial language. In *The Development of Language & Language Researchers: Essays in Honor of Roger Brown.*, Kessel ed. La Jolla, CA: Erlbaum. 1-29.

Bellugi, U. & E. Klima
    1975   Aspects of sign language & its structure. In
    The Role of Speech in Language,
    Kavanagh & Cutting eds. Cambridge, MA:
    MIT Press. 171-205.
Bellugi, U. et al.
    1988   The development of spatialized syntactic
    mechanisms in   American Sign Language.
    In *IV. International Symposium on SL*
    Research, Karlsson ed. 1-10.
Bihrle, A., et al.
    1988   Seeing either the forest or the trees:
    Dissociation In visuo-spatial processing,
    Brain & Cognition. San Diego, CA: Salk
    Institute. 1-12.
Cannon, B.
    [1980   You can't hear me. How can I talk to you?:
    Obstacles to effective communication in
    sign/voice interpreted phone calls.
    Unpublished MS.]
Cokely, D.
    1992   *Interpretation: A Sociolinguistic Model*
    (Sign Language Dissertation Series I).
    Burtonsville, MD: Linstok Press. [Ph.D.
    Dissertation. Georgetown University, 1984].

Dumont, R.

1972   Learning English & how to be silent:
Studies in Sioux & Cherokee classrooms.
In *Functions of Language in the Classroom,*
Cazden ed. NY: Teachers College Press.
344–369.

Goffman, E.

1959   *Presentation of Self in Everyday Life.* NY:
Doubleday.

1981   *Forms of Talk.* Philadelphia: University of
Penn. Press (See "Footing," pp. 124–159).

Gumperz, J.

1982a Discourse *Strategies.* Cambridge
University Press.
1982b Language *& Social Identity.* NY:
Cambridge University Press.

- - - - - & J. Cook-Gumperz

1982   Introduction. In Gumperz 1982b: 1–21.

Gumperz, J. & D. Tannen

1979   Individual & Social Differences in
Language Use. In *Individual Differences in
Language Ability & Language Behavior.*
Fillmore, et al. eds. NY: Academic Press.
305–325.

Johnson, R. & C. Erting
    1984   Linguistic socialization in the context of
    emergent deaf ethnicity,*Working Paper
    Series,* Brukman ed. Wenner-Gren.

Klima, E. et al.
    1979   The structured use of space & movement:
            Morphological processes. In *The Signs of
            Language*, Klima & Bellugi ed. Cambridge,
    MA: Harvard University Press. 272–315.

LeMaster, B.
    1986   Gender sign language difference of Irish
            intriguing, *LINK: Official Publication of the
            National Association of the Deaf*, Dublin.
    1991   Knowing & using female & male signs in
            Dublin, *Sign Language Studies* 73, 361–
            396.

Lillo-Martin, D. et al.
    1983   Processing of spatially organized syntax in
    American Sign Language, Working paper,
    Salk Institute, San Diego. 1–16.

Lillo-Martin, D. et al.
    1985   The acquisition of spatially organized syntax,
    Papers & Reports on Child Language Development, 24,
    70–78.

Markowicz, H. & J. Woodward
1978   Language & the maintenance of ethnic
boundaries in the deaf community,
Communication and Cognition 11, 29–38.
Mather, S.
1987   Eye-gaze & communication a deaf
classroom, *Sign Language Studies* 54,
11–30.
Mohatt, G. & F. Erickson
1981   Cultural differences in teaching styles in an
Odawa school. In *Culture & the Bilingual
Classroom*, Treuba et al. eds. Rowley, MA:
Newbury House. 105–119.
Padden, C.
1980   The deaf community & the culture of deaf
people. *Sign Language & the Deaf
Community,* Baker & Battison eds. Silver
Spring, MD: National Assn. of the Deaf.
Padden, C. & T. Humphries
1988   *Deaf in America: Voices from a Culture.*
Harvard U. Press.
Phillips, S.
1972   Participant structures & communicative
competence. In *Functions of Language in
the Classroom,* Cazden ed. NY: Teachers
College Press. 370–394.

Rasmus, B. & D. Allen

   1988   Testing new signs for teaching biology, *Sign Language Studies* 60, 313–330.

Registry of Interpreters for the Deaf, Inc.

   1980   *Code of Ethics*. Rockville, MD. RID. 2–6.

Scollon, R. & S. Scollon

   1981   Athabaskan-English interethnic communi-
           cation. In *Narrative. Literacy, & Face in Interethnic Interaction*. Norwood, NJ: Ablex Stokoe, W.

   1970   Sign language diglossia, *Studies in Linguistics* 21, 27–41.

Woodward, J.

   1972   Implications for sociolinguistics research
           among the deaf, *Sign Language Studies*
           1, 1–7.

   [1973 Implicational lects on the deaf diglossic
           continuum. Ph.D. dissertation, Georgetown
           University.]

Woodward, J.

  1982   *How You Gonna Get to Heaven if You can't Talk with Jesus: On Depathologizing Deafness*. Silver Spring, MD: T. J. Publishers.

- - - - - & H. Markowicz

  [1975   Some handy new ideas on pidgins & creoles: Pidgin sign languages. Paper presented at the International Conference on Pidgin & Creole Languages. Honolulu.]